LUCINDA GUY

D E   **KIDS**

H   **NGS**

LUCINDA GUY
DESIGNS FOR KIDS
HANDKNITS AND THINGS

Illustrations by François Hall

ROWAN

This book is for Daphne who taught me to knit

A Rowan publication

First published in 2005 by
Rowan Yarns
Green Lane Mill
Holmfirth
West Yorkshire
England
HD9 2DX

Designs by Lucinda Guy
Photography and layout by François Hall
Editor Sally Harding
Pattern writer Eva Yates
Pattern checker Stella Smith

British Library Cataloguing in Publication Data
A catalogue record for this book is available from the
British Library.
ISBN 1 904485 30 8

Printed in Singapore

CONTENTS

INTRODUCTION

The main aim of this book is for you to enjoy knitting some very special and original things that the children in your life will love to wear, love to use and love to play with.

The simple embroidery (ordinary French knots and simple running stitch) that I have used really bring the designs alive and add texture and colour to classic knitwear — this is very much my signature!

All the designs are suitable for the average knitter, and the above average, of course! Some of the pieces are very easy to knit, for example, the Woolly Cap and Scarf (see page 100). They are simply all about the gorgeous colour and feel of the yarn. You will need to work from charts for many of the other designs but these are very straightforward, and if you relax and enjoy it, they will knit up beautifully! You must take time to get the correct tension as it really will make the difference between a superb knit and a disaster. So to get it right, experiment with a test swatch before you start. This applies to the embroidery as well — you do not want floppy French knots or rucked up running stitch.

The book is divided into four sections with garments, accessories, blankets and toys for every season and everything is made with Rowan yarns.

I have used Rowan's *Wool Cotton* for the Spring group because of its superb, fresh colour range and its appropriate wool/cotton combo — warm but fresh *and* machine-washable.

Rowan *Cotton Glace* is an old favourite of mine, and I have used it for the Summer group. It is a sophisticated yarn that knits up nice and finely — not at all chunky — which is ideal for little shoulders and delicate skin. It is practical as well for summer, since it is also machine-washable.

The Autumn group is knitted in Rowan's *4ply Soft* which gives a classic, lightweight finish that is perfect for layers of warmth! Again, this yarn is machine-washable, ensuring essential woolly items that are easy to keep clean.

I had cosy, sumptuous softness in mind for the Winter group and so have used Rowan *Kid Classic*. The jewel-like colours and serious cosiness of this yarn made it the obvious choice for beating any winter blues. You will need to hand wash anything knit from this chapter as the yarn is very special and very delicate.

When washing any of the knits and things from this book, whether machine- or hand-washable, I would advise you to treat them carefully. Always turn items inside out to protect the embroidery and use a very gentle detergent. A good-quality gentle shampoo works very well with delicate and treasured handknits when you hand wash. Hand-washed knits can be rolled up carefully in a clean towel to remove excess water. If you are going to spin dry, put the knits into a clean pillowcase first. Always dry your knits flat and away from direct sunlight. When they are dry then you can put them out to air!

Treat these very special handknits and things with a lot of care and they will last you a lifetime and even into future generations!

Start knitting your heirlooms now!

HANDSOME HOUND

Handsome Hound is the perfect companion for a spring walk. Tuck him under your arm and set off to find some nice big puddles to play in.

BEFORE YOU BEGIN

YARN

Height, excluding tail   15cm (6in)

Rowan Wool Cotton
MC Main colour   2 x 50g
CC Contrasting colour   1 x 50g

Washable stuffing.

NEEDLES

1 pair of 4.5mm (US 7) needles.
Spare needle.

TENSION

20 sts and 27 rows = 10cm (4in) square measured over stocking stitch using 4.5mm (US 7) needles.

SPECIAL NOTE

Work in stocking stitch (knit all RS rows and purl all WS rows) throughout.

GETTING STARTED

BODY SIDE 1 Ⓐ

Using 4.5mm (US 7) needles and yarn MC, cast on 18 sts for back leg. Work 11 rows in st st, inc 1 st at END of rows 5 and 9. 20 sts. Leave sts on spare needle.
Using 4.5mm (US 7) needles and yarn MC, cast on 15 sts for front leg. Work 11 rows in st st, inc 1 st at each end of rows 5 and 8. 19 sts.
Row 12 Inc, P18, cast on 15 sts, P across 20 sts on spare needle.
Rows 13 to 62 Follow chart 1 (see page 12).

BODY SIDE 2 Ⓑ

Using 4.5mm (US 7) needles and yarn MC, cast on 15 sts for front leg. Work 11 rows in st st, inc 1 st at each end of rows 5 and 8. 19 sts. Leave sts on spare needle.
Using 4.5mm (US 7) needles and yarn MC, cast

on 18 sts for back leg. Work 11 rows in st st, inc 1 st at BEG of rows 5 and 9. 20 sts.
Row 12 P20, cast on 15 sts, from spare needle P18, inc.
Rows 13 to 62 Follow chart 2 (see page 12).

UNDERBODY Ⓒ

Using 4.5mm (US 7) needles and yarn MC, cast on 19 sts for back leg. Work 11 rows in st st, inc 1 st at END of row 9. 20 sts. Leave sts on spare needle.
Using 4.5mm (US 7) needles and yarn MC, cast on 17 sts for front leg. Work 11 rows in st st, inc 1 st at each end of row 8. 19 sts.
Row 12 Inc, P18, cast on 15 sts, P across 20 sts on spare needle.
Rows 13 to 44 Follow chart 3 (see page 13).

OUTER EAR Ⓓ

Using 4.5mm (US 7) needles and yarn CC, cast on 15 sts and follow chart 4 (see page 13). Make second outer ear.

INNER EAR Ⓔ

Using 4.5mm (US 7) needles and yarn MC, cast on 15 sts and follow chart 5. Make second inner ear.

MAKING UP

Press all pieces on WS using a warm iron over a damp cloth. Using yarn CC, embroider paws with large straight sts and make a 10-loop French knot for each eye as marked.

With RS facing, join an inner ear to an outer ear, noting there will be a 5-row extension at base of outer ear. Turn RS out and stuff. Close ear leaving 5-row flap. Repeat for second ear. Place ears with brown sides together and backstitch cast-on edges.

With RS together, pin main body from nose to tail, placing ears (joined 5-row flap) as marked

chart 1

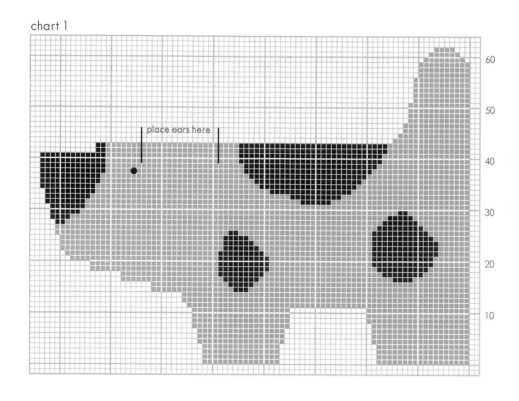

place ears here

60
50
40
30
20
10

chart 2

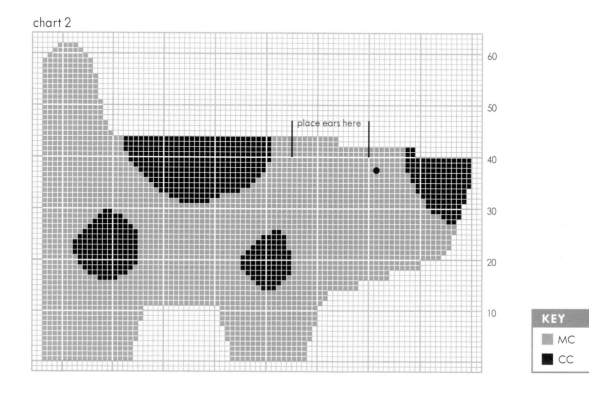

place ears here

60
50
40
30
20
10

KEY	
	MC
	CC

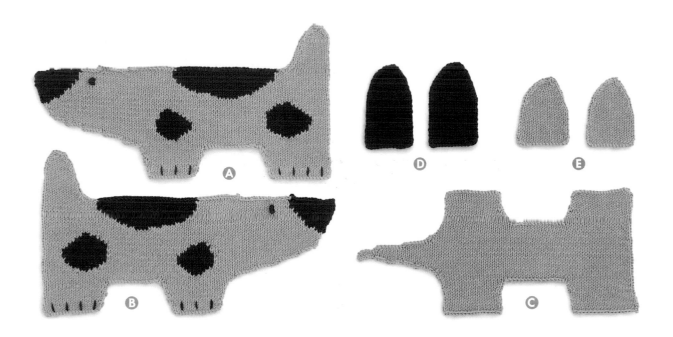

chart 3

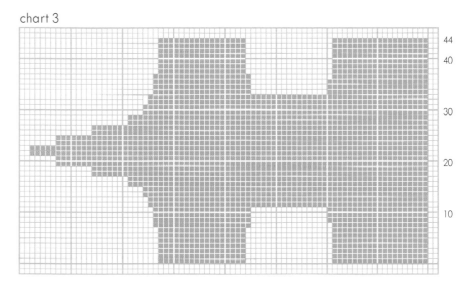

	44
	40
	30
	20
	10

chart 4

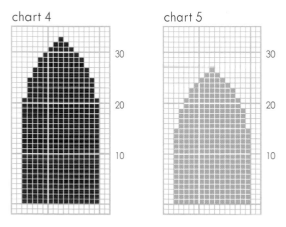

	30
	20
	10

chart 5

	30
	20
	10

on chart and noting ears must be facing down and like 'the filling in a sandwich'. Sew body, starting at nose and working towards tail. Stitch length of tail and leave a long loose end. Stitch straight edge of undernose for about 2cm (¾in), then pin underbody into position. Backstitch in place, leaving about 7cm (2¾in) open at tail end. Turn Handsome Hound RS out. Stuff carefully, then close opening neatly.

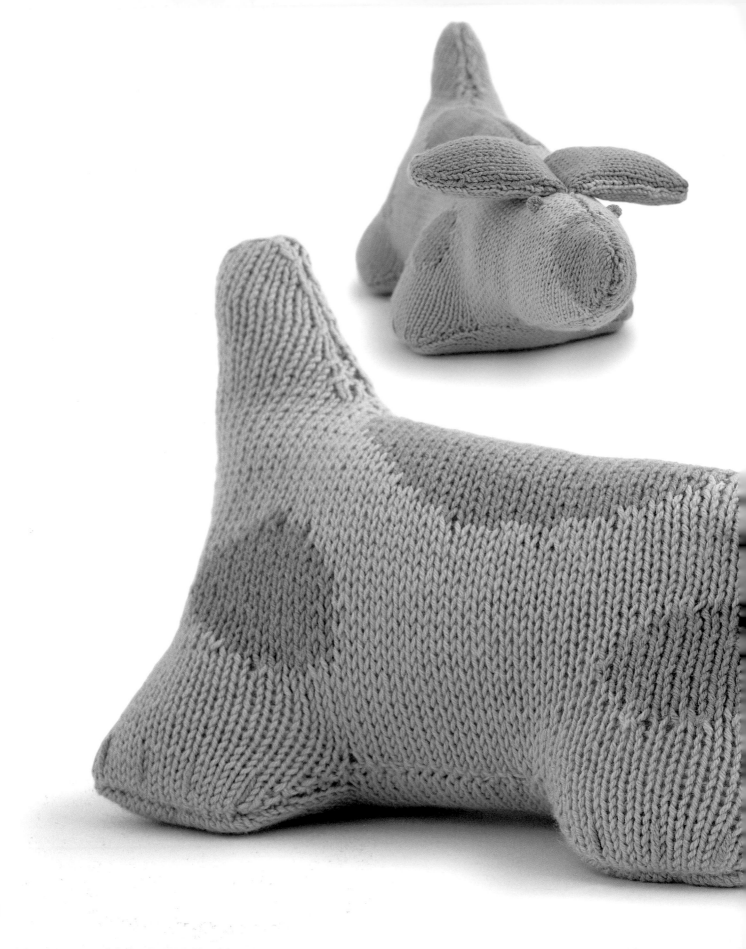

HAPPY HEN SWEATER

Wear this Happy Hen Sweater at an egg hunt and you can keep the smaller eggs in the handy pocket!

BEFORE YOU BEGIN

YARN

Size	2-3 yrs	3-4 yrs	4-5 yrs
To fit chest	56cm	61cm	66cm
	22in	24in	26in
Actual size	74cm	78cm	82cm
	29in	31in	32½in
Back length	36cm	38cm	40cm
	14in	15in	16in
Underarm seam	22cm	23cm	24cm
	8½in	9in	9½in

Rowan Wool Cotton	2-3 yrs	3-4 yrs	4-5 yrs
A Pale pink (951)	3	4	4 x 50g
B Olive green (946)	3	3	4 x 50g
C Red (957)	1	1	1 x 50g

Small amounts of turquoise (949) and off-white (900) for embroidery.

NEEDLES

1 pair of 4mm (US 6) needles.
Cable needle.

TENSION

22 sts and 30 rows = 10cm (4in) square measured over stocking stitch using 4mm (US 6) needles.
22 sts and 38 rows = 10cm (4in) square measured over garter stitch using 4mm (US 6) needles.

SPECIAL ABBREVIATION

c3L = slip first stitch onto cable needle and leave at front of work, K2, K1 from cable needle.

GETTING STARTED

BACK

Using 4mm (US 6) needles and yarn A, cast on 83 (87: 91) sts and work border as follows:
Row 1 (RS) K0 (2: 4), *sl1, K7, rep from * to last 3 (5: 7) sts, sl1, K2 (4: 6).
Row 2 K0 (2: 4), *P2, sl1, K5, rep from * to last 3 (5: 7) sts, P2, sl1, K0 (2: 4).
Row 3 K0 (2: 4), *c3L, K5, rep from * to last 3 (5: 7) sts, c3L, K0 (2: 4).
Row 4 K0 (2: 4), *P3, K5, rep from * to last 3 (5: 7) sts, P3, K0 (2: 4).
Work rows 1 to 4 again.
Change to st st and, using intarsia method, work as follows:
Row 9 K8 (10: 12) B, *sl1, 2A, 29B, rep from *, to last 11 (13: 15) sts, sl1, 2A, 8 (10: 12) B.
Row 10 P8 (10: 12) B, *2A, sl1, 29B, rep from * to last 11 (13: 15) sts, 2A, sl1, 8 (10: 12) B.
Row 11 K8 (10: 12) B, *c3LA, 29B, rep from * to last 11 (13: 15) sts, c3LA, 8 (10: 12) B.
Row 12 P8 (10: 12) B, *3A, 29B, rep from * to last 11 (13: 15) sts, 3A, 8 (10: 12) B.**
Rows 9 to 12 form panel patt. Cont in panel patt until work meas 21 (22.5: 24) cm [8¼ (8¾: 9¼) in], ending with RS facing for next row.
Change to yarn A and g st (every row, knit).
Work 2 rows.

Shape armholes

Cast off 2 sts beg of next 6 rows. 71 (75: 79) sts.***
Cont in g st until work meas 36 (38: 40) cm [14 (15: 16) in], ending with RS facing for next row.

Shape shoulders and neck

Row 1 Cast off 7 (8: 9) sts, K16, cast off 25 (27: 29) sts, K23 (24: 25).
Work first side on 23 (24: 25) sts as follows:
Row 2 Cast off 7 (8: 9) sts, K to end.
Row 3 Cast off 5 sts.
Cast off rem 11 sts.
Rejoin yarn to rem sts at neck edge and work to match first side.

FRONT

Work as for back to ** (completion of row 12).
Work 4 rows more in panel patt.
Place hen chart as follows:

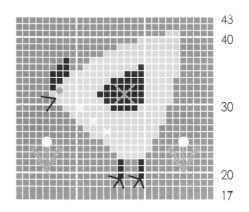
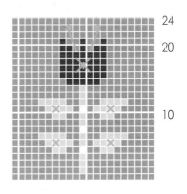
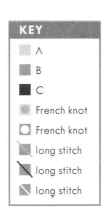

KEY

⋀	A
■	B
■	C
●	French knot
○	French knot
⧄	long stitch
⧅	long stitch
⧄	long stitch

Row 17 Patt 11 (13: 15), work row 17 from hen chart, patt to end.

Rows 18 to 43 Patt and complete hen. Cont as for back to ***.

Divide for neck

Next row K35 (37: 39), cast off 1 st, K to end.

Work first side of neck on 35 (37: 39) sts as follows:

Row 1 K to last 3 sts, K2tog, K1.

Row 2 K1, sl1, K1, psso, K to end.

Rep rows 1 and 2, 3 times.

Dec 1 st at neck edge on next 4 alt rows. 23 (25: 27) sts.

Dec 1 st at neck edge on every foll 4th row until 18 (19: 20) sts rem. Cont without shaping until work meas 36 (38: 40) cm [14 (15: 16) in], ending with WS facing for next row.

Shape shoulders

Next row Cast off 7 (8: 9) sts, K to end.

Work 1 row. Cast off rem 11 sts.

With WS facing, rejoin yarn to rem sts at neck edge and work to match first side, reversing all shaping.

SLEEVES

Using 4mm (US 6) needles and yarn A, cast on 41 (43: 45) sts and work as follows:

Row 1 K3 (4: 5), *sl1, K7, rep from * to last 6 (7: 8) sts, sl1, K5 (6: 7).

Rows 2 to 8 Using row 1 for placement of cables, complete as border on back.

Change to yarn B and g st. Inc 1 st at each end of every 5th row to 65 (69: 73) sts. Cont without shaping until work meas 22 (23: 24) cm [8½ (9: 9½) in].

Shape sleevehead

Cast off 2 sts at beg of next 6 rows. Cast off.

POCKET

Using 4mm (US 6) needles and yarn B, cast on 21 sts. Working in st st, follow flower chart. Change to yarn A and K 6 rows. Cast off.

EMBROIDERY

Press all pieces lightly on WS using a warm iron over a damp cloth. Embroider details as indicated on flower and hen charts.

NECKBAND

Join right shoulder seam. With RS facing and using 4mm (US 6) needles and yarn B, pick up and knit 27 (29: 31) sts down left side of front neck, 1 st from centre front neck, 27 (29: 31) sts up right side of front neck and 35 (37: 39) sts from back neck. Knit 3 rows. Cast off.

MAKING UP

Weave in any loose ends. Join left shoulder seam and neckband. Join side and sleeve seams. Ease sleevehead into armhole and sew into place. Pin pocket to front, with lower edge of pocket level with hen's feet (see page 17), and stitch into place. Press seams, avoiding any embroidery.

DANGEROUS DINOSAUR

Get fierce and hunt for fossils with Dangerous Dinosaur – you might find some of his ancestors!

BEFORE YOU BEGIN

YARN

Size	2-3 yrs	3-4 yrs	4-5 yrs
To fit chest	56cm	61cm	66cm
	22in	24in	26in
Actual size	75.5cm	79cm	83cm
	29½in	31in	32½in
Back length	37cm	39cm	41cm
	14½in	15¼in	16in
Underarm seam	22cm	23cm	24cm
	8½in	9in	9½in

Rowan Wool Cotton	2-3 yrs	3-4 yrs	4-5 yrs
A Turquoise (949)	3	4	4 x 50g
B Dark brown (956)	2	3	3 x 50g
C Olive green (946)	1	1	1 x 50g
D Terracotta (947)	1	1	1 x 50g
E Beige (929)	1	1	1 x 50g

NEEDLES

1 pair of 4mm (US 6) needles.
Stitch holder.

TENSION

22 sts and 30 rows = 10cm (4in) square measured over stocking stitch using 4mm (US 6) needles.

GETTING STARTED

BACK

Using 4mm (US 6) needles and yarn B, cast on 81 (87: 93) sts and work in 3 x 3 rib as follows:

Row 1 *K3, P3, rep from * to last 3 sts, K3.
Row 2 *P3, K3, rep from * to last 3 sts, P3.
Rows 3 to 6 As rows 1 and 2, twice, inc 1 st at each end of last row on Size 1 and dec 1 st at each end of last row on Size 3. 83 (87: 91) sts.
Change to st st and work in stripe patt as follows:
Rows 1 and 2 Yarn A.
Rows 3 and 4 Yarn B.
Rows 5 and 6 Yarn C.
Rows 1 to 6 form stripe patt.

Cont in patt to completion of row 42 (48: 54). Change to broken stripe in st st and work as follows:
Row 1 Yarn A.
Row 2 *1B, 1A, rep from * to last st, 1B.
Rows 3 and 4 Yarn B.
Row 5 *1A, 1B, rep from * to last st, 1A.
Row 6 Yarn A.
Place dinosaur chart (see page 22) as follows:
Row 1 Using yarn A, K14 (16: 18), work 56 sts from row 1 of dinosaur chart, K13 (15: 17).
Rows 2 to 10 Cont with dinosaur chart.

Shape armholes

Rows 11 to 16 Cast off 2 sts at beg of rows, cont with dinosaur. 71 (75: 79) sts.
Rows 17 to 32 Complete dinosaur.
Cont in st st using yarn A until work meas 36 (38: 40) cm [14 (14¾: 15½) in], ending with RS facing for next row.

Shape shoulders and neck

Row 1 Cast off 7 (8: 9) sts, K16, cast off 25 (27: 29) sts, K23 (24: 25).
Work first side on 23 (24: 25) sts as follows:
Row 2 Cast off 7 (8: 9) sts, work to end.
Row 3 Cast off 5 sts, work to end.
Cast off rem 11 sts.
With WS facing, rejoin yarn to rem sts at neck edge and work to match first side, reversing all shaping.

FRONT

Work as for back to completion of dinosaur. Cont in st st until work is 14 (16: 16) rows *less* than back at shoulder, ending with RS facing for next row.

Shape neck

Row 1 K28 (30: 31), turn and work on these sts.
Row 2 P1, P2tog, P to end.

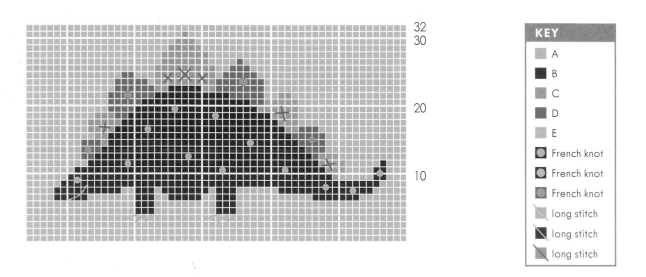

32
30

20

10

Row 3 K to last 3 sts, sl1, K1, psso, K1.
Rows 4 to 7 As rows 2 and 3, twice.
Row 8 P to end.
Rows 9 to 14 As rows 7 and 8, 3 times.
Sizes 2 and 3, work rows 7 and 8 again.

Shape shoulder
Row 1 Cast off 7 (8: 9) sts, K to last 3 sts, sl1, K1, psso, K1.
Row 2 P to end.
Cast off.
Place centre 15 (15: 17) sts on holder.
With RS facing, rejoin yarn to rem sts at neck edge and work to match first side, reversing all shaping.

SLEEVES

Using 4mm (US 6) needles and yarn C, cast on 45 (51: 51) sts and work 6 rows in 3 x 3 rib as on back. Change to yarn B and st st. Inc 1 st at each end of 3rd and every foll 4th row to 65 (69: 73) sts. Cont without shaping until work meas 17 (18: 19) cm [6½ (7: 7½) in], ending with RS facing for next row.
Join in yarn A and work rows 1 to 6 of broken stripe patt. Work 10 rows in yarn A.

Shape sleevehead
Cast off 2 sts at beg of next 6 rows. Cast off.

NECKBAND

Join right shoulder seam. With RS facing and using 4mm (US 6) needles and yarn A, pick up and knit 17 (19: 20) sts down left side of front neck, knit across 15 (15: 17) sts on holder, pick up and knit 17 (19: 20) sts up right side of neck and 35 (37: 39) sts from back neck. 84 (90: 96) sts.
Work 4 rows in 3 x 3 rib. Cast off in rib.

EMBROIDERY

Press all pieces lightly on WS using a warm iron over a damp cloth.
Embroider dinosaur as indicated on chart.

MAKING UP

Weave in any loose ends. Join left shoulder seam and neckband. Join side and sleeve seams. Ease sleevehead into armhole and sew into place. Press seams, avoiding embroidery.

FLOWER TOGGLE HAT

This little hat is great for keeping fresh spring breezes away from your ears.

BEFORE YOU BEGIN

YARN

To fit	2-3 yrs	3-4 yrs	4-5 yrs
Circumference	44cm	46cm	48cm
	17in	18in	19in
Depth	17cm	18cm	19cm
	6in	7in	7in

Rowan Wool Cotton	2-3 yrs	3-4 yrs	4-5 yrs
A Pale pink (951)	1	1	1 x 50g
B Olive green (946)	1	1	1 x 50g

Small amounts of C red (957) and
D pale yellow (942), for flower stamens.

NEEDLES

1 pair of 4mm (US 6) needles.

TENSION

22 sts and 30 rows = 10cm (4in) square measured over stocking stitch using 4mm (US 6) needles.

GETTING STARTED

HAT

Using 4mm (US 6) needles and yarn A, cast on 49 (52: 55) sts and work as follows:
Row 1 (WS) K1 (0: 3), *P1, K3, rep from * to end.
Row 2 K to end.
Rep rows 1 and 2 twice and then row 1 again. Change to yarn B and cont in patt until work measures 12 (13: 14) cm [4½ (5: 5½) in], ending with row 1 of patt.

Shape top

Row 1 *K2tog K2, rep from * to last 1 (0: 3) sts, K1 (0: K2tog, K1)
Row 2 K1 (0: 2), *P1, K2, rep from * to end.
Row 3 K to end.
Row 4 As row 2.
Row 5 *K2tog, K1, rep from * to last 1 (0: 2) sts, K1 (0: K2tog).
Row 6 P0 (1: 0) *K1, P1, rep from * to last st, K1.
Row 7 K to end.

Rows 8 and 9 As rows 6 and 7.
Row 10 P2tog across row to last 1 (0: 1) st, P1 (0: 1).
Row 11 K to end.
Row 12 P2tog across row to last 1 (1: 0) st, P1 (1: 0).
Row 13 K to end.
Row 14 P2tog across row to last st, P1.
Row 15 K to end.
Cast off.

FLOWER TOGGLE

Using 4mm (US 6) needles and yarn A, cast on 29 sts and work as follows:
Row 1 (RS) K1, *P3, K1, rep from * to end.
Row 2 P to end.
Rows 3 to 8 As rows 1 and 2, 3 times.
Row 9 K1, *P2tog, P1, K1, rep from * to end.
Row 10 P to end.
Row 11 K1, *P2tog, K1, rep from * to end.
Row 12 P to end.
Row 13 K3tog across row. 5 sts.
Work 11 rows in st st. Cast off, leaving a long loose end for sewing.

MAKING UP
Flower toggle

To make stamens, cut three 20cm (8in) lengths of yarn C and three 15cm (6in) lengths of yarn D. Fold stamens in half and lay inside toggle with loops at cast-off edge. Fold toggle around stamens and, with long loose end for sewing, catch loop ends of stamens to toggle, then carefully sew toggle side edges together. Make a knot at required length on each stamen and trim.

Hat

With RS facing, join side edges of hat, leaving small opening at top of hat. Turn hat RS out. Insert toggle in opening and sew in place.
(For posy instructions, see page 28.)

FLOWER POSY

A perfect accessory for your spring coat. Wear it with the Flower Toggle Hat and you will look very stylish.

BEFORE YOU BEGIN

YARN
Rowan Wool Cotton

A Pale pink (951)	1 x 50g
B Pale yellow (942)	1 x 50g
C Red (957)	1 x 50g

Brooch pin (optional).

NEEDLES
1 pair each of 3.25mm (US 3) and 4mm (US 6) needles.

TENSION
22 sts and 30 rows = 10cm (4in) square measured over stocking stitch using 4mm (US 6) needles.

GETTING STARTED

FLOWER
Using 4mm (US 6) needles and yarn A, cast on 29 sts and work as follows:
Row 1 (RS) K1, *P3, K1, rep from * to end.
Row 2 P to end.
Rows 3 to 8 As rows 1 and 2, 3 times.
Row 9 K1, *P2tog, P1, K1, rep from * to end.
Row 10 P to end.
Row 11 K1, *P2tog, K1, rep from * to end.
Row 12 P to end.
Row 13 K3tog across row.
Work 11 rows in st st. Cast off, leaving a long loose end for sewing.
Make two more flowers in same way, one in yarn A and one in yarn B.

BOW
Using 3.25mm (US 3) needles and yarn C, cast on 3 sts and work in g st (every row, knit) for 25cm (10in). Cast off.

CENTRE KNOT
Using 3.25mm (US 3) needles and yarn C, cast on 2 sts and work in g st for 2.5cm (1in). Cast off.

ATTACHING BAND
Using 3.25mm (US 3) needles and yarn C, cast on 3 sts and work in g st for 4cm (1½in). Cast off.

MAKING UP
Flower

To make stamens, cut three 20cm (8in) lengths of yarn C and three 15cm (6in) lengths of yarn B — use yarn A in yarn-B flower. Fold stamens in half and lay inside toggle with loops at cast-off edge. Fold toggle around stamens and, with long loose end for sewing, catch loop ends of stamens to toggle, then carefully sew toggle side edges together. Make a knot at required length on each stamen and trim.

Form bow and pin, then stitch 'knot' around bow. Pin bow into place and stitch securely to attaching band. Place flowers together and secure with attaching band. If desired, sew a brooch pin to back of posy.

(**Note** To make two-flower posy on pages 3, 5 and 101, follow these same instructions, but use Rowan *Kid Classic* in desired shades.)

PATCHWORK BLANKET

Take this beautiful blanket on your first picnic of the year and you will be as snug as all the spring lambs in their curly coats.

BEFORE YOU BEGIN

YARN

Size, excluding edging	91 x 91cm	
	36 x 36in	

Rowan Wool Cotton

A Olive green (946)	10 x 50g
B Pale yellow (942)	4 x 50g
C Pale pink (951)	1 x 50g
D Pale blue (941)	1 x 50g

NEEDLES

1 pair of 4mm (US 6) needles.

TENSION

22 sts and 38 rows = 10cm (4in) square measured over garter stitch using 4mm (US 6) needles.

GETTING STARTED

PLAIN SQUARE Ⓐ

Using 4mm (US 6) needles and yarn A, cast on 30 sts and work 50 rows in g st (every row, knit). Cast off. Make 23 squares more in same way (for 24 in total).

STRIPED SQUARE 1 Ⓑ

Using 4mm (US 6) needles and yarn B, cast on 30 sts and work in g st stripes as follows:
Rows 1 and 2 Yarn B.
Rows 3 and 4 Yarn A.
Rows 5 and 6 Yarn B.
Rows 7 and 8 Yarn C.
Rows 9 to 48 As rows 1 to 8, 5 times.
Rows 49 and 50 Yarn B.
Cast off.
Make 12 squares more in same way (for 13 in total).

STRIPED SQUARE 2 Ⓒ

Make 12 squares in total, working as for striped square 1 BUT using yarn D for yarn C.

EDGING

Using 4mm (US 6) needles and yarn A, cast on 8 sts and work as follows:
Row 1 K4, yon, K2tog, yon, K2.
Row 2 K to end.
Row 3 K4, yon, K2tog, K1, yon, K2.
Row 4 K to end.
Row 5 K4, yon, K2tog, K2, yon, K2.
Row 6 K to end.
Row 7 K4, yon, K2tog, K3, yon, K2.
Row 8 K to end.
Row 9 K4, yon, K2tog, K4, yon, K2.
Row 10 K to end.
Row 11 K4, yon, K2tog, K5, yon, K2.
Row 12 Cast off 6 sts, K to end.
Rows 1 to 12 form patt rep. Cont in patt until edging fits easily around blanket. Cast off.

MAKING UP

Join squares together as diagram, ensuring that squares are RS together before stitching (use backstitch for strength). Attach edging to blanket, easing around corners. Press lightly using a warm iron over a damp cloth.

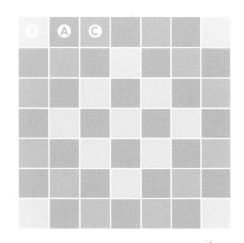

SUMMER

BIRDIE

Birdie loves the summertime as he originally comes from hot volcanic islands in a far away place. His foolish expression is due to too much sun.

YARN

Beak to tail	24cm (9½in)
Height	13cm (5in)

Rowan Cotton Glace

MC Main colour	1 x 50g
CC Contrasting colour	1 x 50g

Washable stuffing.

NEEDLES

1 pair of 3.25mm (US 3) needles.
2mm (US B1) crochet hook.

TENSION

24 sts and 34 rows = 10cm (4in) square measured over stocking stitch using 3.25mm (US 3) needles.

GETTING STARTED

MAIN BODY Ⓐ

Using 3.25mm (US 3) needles and yarn MC, cast on 34 sts and work as follows:

Rows 1 to 16 St st.
Row 17 K1, sl1, K1, psso, K to last 3 sts, K2tog, K1.
Rows 18 to 23 St st.
Row 24 P1, P2tog, P to last 3 sts, P2tog tbl, P1.
Rows 25 and 26 St st.
Row 27 As row 17.
Row 28 P to end.
Rows 29 to 40 As rows 27 and 28, 6 times. 16 sts.
Cast off.
Make second main body piece.

UNDERBODY Ⓑ

Using 3.25mm (US 3) needles and yarn CC, cast on 4 sts (this is tail end) and work as follows:

Rows 1 to 3 St st.
Row 4 Inc, P to last 2 sts, inc, P1.
Rows 5 and 6 St st.

Row 7 Inc, K to last 2 sts, inc, K1.
Rows 8 to 13 St st.
Row 14 As row 4.
Rows 15 and 16 St st.
Row 17 As row 7.
Row 18 P to end.
Rows 19 to 22 As rows 17 and 18, twice.
Rows 23 to 60 St st.
Row 61 K1, sl1, K1, psso, K to last 3 sts, K2tog, K1.
Row 62 P to end.
Rows 63 to 72 As rows 61 and 62, 5 times. 4 sts.
Row 73 K2tog twice, pass the first stitch over the second st. Fasten off.

BEAK Ⓒ

Using 3.25mm (US 3) needles and yarn CC, cast on 15 sts and work as follows:

Rows 1 and 2 St st.
Row 3 K1, sl1, K1, psso, K to last 3 sts, K2tog, K1.
Row 4 P to end.
Rows 5 to 12 As rows 3 and 4, 4 times. 5 sts.
Row 13 K1, sl1, K2tog, psso, K1.
Row 14 P to end.
Row 15 K3tog. Fasten off.
Make second beak piece.

TAIL Ⓓ

Using 3.25mm (US 3) needles and yarn MC, cast on 6 sts and work as follows:

Row 1 K to end.
Row 2 Inc, P to last 2 sts, inc, P1.
Row 3 Inc, K to last 2 sts, inc, K1.
Rows 4 and 5 As rows 2 and 3.
Row 6 As row 2. 16 sts.
Rows 7 to 11 St st.
Row 12 (P2tog, P3) twice, P2tog, P2, P2tog. 12 sts.

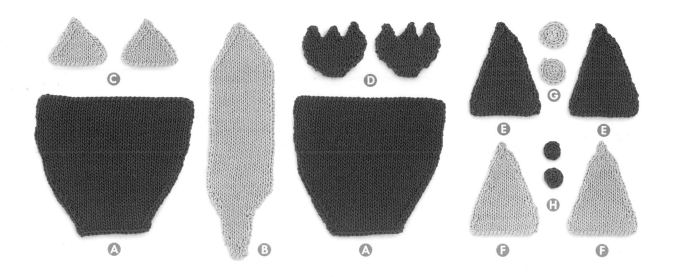

Shape tail

Row 13 K4, turn, P2tog twice, turn, K2, turn, P2, turn, K2tog. Fasten off.

(Rejoin yarn to rem sts, work row 13 and fasten off) twice.

Make second tail piece.

TOP OF WING E

Using 3.25mm (US 3) needles and yarn MC, cast on 17 sts and work as follows:

Rows 1 to 4 St st.

Row 5 K1, sl1, K1, psso, K to last 3 sts, K2tog, K1.

Rows 6 to 9 St st.

Row 10 P1, P2tog, P to last 3 sts, P2tog tbl, P1.

Rows 11 to 15 As rows 1 to 5.

Rows 16 and 17 St st.

Row 18 As row 10.

Row 19 to 21 St st.

Row 22 As row 10.

Row 23 K to end.

Rows 24 and 25 As rows 22 and 23.

Row 26 P1, P3tog, P1.

Row 27 K to end.

Row 28 P3tog. Fasten off.

Make second wing top.

UNDERSIDE OF WING F

Using 3.25mm (US 3) needles and yarn CC, cast on 17 sts and work as for top of wing.

Make second wing underside.

MAIN EYE G

Make main eye in double crochet (US single crochet) as follows:

Using 2mm (US B1) crochet hook and yarn CC, make 3 chain and join with a slip stitch in first chain to form a ring.

Round 1 6dc into ring.

Round 2 *1dc into each of next 2dc, 2dc into next dc, rep from * once more. 8dc.**

Round 3 *1dc into each of next 3dc, 2dc into next dc, rep from * once more. 10dc.

Round 4 *1dc into each of next 4dc, 2dc into next dc, rep from * once more. 12dc.

Fasten off, leaving a long loose end for sewing.

Make second main eye piece.

CENTRE OF EYE H

Using 2mm (US B1) crochet hook and yarn MC, make as for main eye to ** and fasten off, leaving a long loose end for sewing.

Make second eye centre.

MAKING UP

Press all pieces on WS using a warm iron over a damp cloth.

Beak

Place RS of two beak pieces together and backstitch around beak, leaving cast-on edges open for stuffing.

Wings

Place a wing piece in yarn MC together with a wing piece in yarn CC, with RS facing. Backstitch around wing, leaving cast-on edges open for stuffing. Stitch second wing to match. Turn RS out and stuff wings to a uniform thickness of about 28mm (1⅛in). Backstitch final seam, leaving a long loose end for attaching wing to body.

Tail

Place RS of two pieces together and backstitch around tail, leaving cast-on edges open for stuffing. Turn RS out and, using the round end of a knitting needle, gently ease tail into shape, ensuring that it has three nice 'peaks'.

Eyes

Place a centre eye on top of a main eye as shown, to create bird's foolish expression, and stitch into position. Stitch second eye to match.

Body

Place RS of two pieces of main body together and backstitch along straight edge. Press this seam. Turn back RS out and stuff to a uniform thickness of about 25mm (1in). With RS facing and ensuring that beak seam is matched to body seam, pin straight edge of beak to main body and backstitch into position. Stuff tail to a uniform thickness of about 24mm (⅞in). Attach tail to other end of body in same way.

Underbody

With RS of body and underbody facing, and ensuring that tail end of underbody matches tail end of bird, pin underbody in place. Starting at one side of tail, backstitch around, leaving about 3cm (1¼in) open below tail on other side. Turn RS out and stuff to a uniform thickness of about 7.5cm (3in).
Finish sewing underbody to main body.
Attach eyes and wings to body as shown, sewing both sides of wings to secure them well.

FANTASTIC FLOWER FROCK

Truly gorgeous the Fantastic Flower Frock is the essential summer dress for your birthday teas and garden parties.

YARN

Size	2-3 yrs	3-4 yrs	4-5 yrs
To fit chest	56cm	61cm	66cm
	22in	24in	26in
Actual size	62cm	66cm	70cm
	24½ in	26in	27½in
Back length	45cm	47cm	49cm
	18in	18½in	19½in
Sleeve seam	7cm	7cm	7cm
	2½in	2½in	2½in

Rowan Cotton Glace	2-3 yrs	3-4 yrs	4-5 yrs
A Red (741)	2	3	3 x 50g
B Pink (747 or 799)	3	3	4 x 50g
C Turquoise (809)	1	1	1 x 50g
D Pale green (813)	1	1	1 x 50g

NEEDLES

1 pair of 3.75mm (US 5) needles.
2mm (US B1) and 3mm (US D3) crochet hooks.
Stitch holders.

TENSION

23 sts and 32 rows = 10cm (4in) square measured over stocking stitch using 3.75mm (US 5) needles.
26 sts and 32 rows = 10cm (4in) square measured over textured stitch using 3.75mm (US 5) needles.

FRONT

Using 3.75mm (US 5) needles and yarn A, cast on 101 (107: 111) sts and work textured stitch as follows:
Rows 1 and 2 K to end.
Row 3 (RS) P1, *K1, P1, rep from * to end.
Row 4 K1, *P1, K1, rep from * to end.
Rep rows 1 to 4 once more, ending last row P2tog. 100 (106: 110) sts.
Change to yarn B and st st. Work rows 1 to 86 from chart (see page 47), working decs on RS rows as K1, sl1, K1, psso, K to last 3 sts, K2tog, K1 and on WS rows as P1, P2tog, P to last 3 sts, P2tog tbl, P1 AND on row 86, inc 1 st at end of row. 81 (87: 91) sts. Break yarn B.
Change to yarn A and work 6 (10: 14) rows in textured stitch.

Shape armholes

Row 1 K1, sl1, K1, psso, patt to last 3 sts, K2tog, K1.
Row 2 Patt.
Rep rows 1 and 2 to 65 (69: 73) sts.***
Work 12 (10: 12) rows more, ending with RS facing for next row.

Shape neck

Next row Patt 27 (28: 30) sts, turn.
Keeping patt correct, work on these sts as follows:
Row 1 (WS) Cast off 2 sts, patt to end.
Dec 1 st at neck edge on next and foll alt rows to 20 (21: 22) sts. Work 5 (7: 5) rows more.
Cast off.
Rejoin yarn to rem sts and cast off centre 11 (13: 13) sts, patt to end.
Work rem sts to match first side of neck, reversing shaping.

BACK

Work as for front to *** (completion of armhole shaping).
Work 8 rows more in patt, ending with RS facing for next row.

Divide for back opening

Next row Patt 31 (33: 35) sts, cast off 3 sts, patt 31 (33: 35) sts.
Working first side on 31 (33: 35) sts, work 17 (17: 19) rows in patt.

Shape neck

Row 1 Cast off 6 (7: 8) sts, patt to end.
Row 2 Patt.
Row 3 Cast off 5 sts, patt to end.
Cast off.
Rejoin yarn to rem sts and work to match first side of opening, reversing all shaping.

SLEEVES

Using 3.75mm (US 5) needles and yarn A, cast on 47 (49: 51) sts and work 8 rows in textured stitch. Inc 1 st at each end of next and every foll alt row to 61 (63: 65) sts. Work 2 rows more.

Shape sleevehead

Rows 1 and 2 Cast off 2 sts, patt to end.
Rows 3 and 4 Cast off 4 sts, patt to end.
Rows 5 and 6 Cast off 4 (5: 5) sts, patt to end.
Cast off.

EMBROIDERY

Press front and back lightly on WS using a warm iron over a damp cloth. Embroider details as indicated on chart.

MAKING UP

Weave in any loose ends. Join shoulder seams. Join side and sleeve seams. Ease sleevehead into armhole and sew into place.

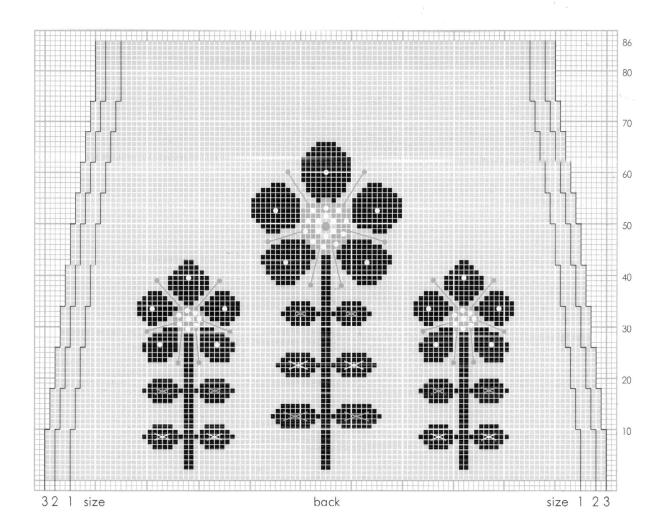

3 2 1 size   back   size 1 2 3

Crochet picot edging

Using a 3mm (US D3) crochet hook and yarn C, work a double crochet (US single crochet) and picot edging evenly around bottom of dress, sleeves, neck and back neck opening as follows:

Picot round (RS) *Work 3dc, make 3 chain and join with a slip stitch in last dc to form picot, rep from *.

Crochet button and button loop

Using a 2mm (US B1) crochet hook and yarn A, work a double crochet (US single crochet) button as follows:

Make 3 chain and join with a slip stitch in first chain to form a ring.

Round 1 6dc into ring.

Round 2 1dc into each dc.

Round 3 *1dc into next dc, draw a loop through each of next 2dc, draw a loop through all 3 loops on hook, rep from * once more. 4dc. Fasten off, leaving a long loose end. Weave loose end through edge, pull to gather, and secure.

Sew button into place at top of back opening, then work a 4-chain loop for buttonhole on opposite side of opening.

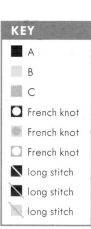

KEY	
■	A
▢	B
▨	C
◘	French knot
●	French knot
◻	French knot
◣	long stitch
◥	long stitch
◸	long stitch

FANTASTIC FLOWER CAP

Complete the gorgeousness of the Flower Frock outfit with this little cap!

YARN

To fit	2-3 yrs	3-4 yrs	4-5 yrs
Circumference	44cm	46cm	48cm
	17½in	18in	19in
Depth	17cm	18cm	19cm
	6½in	7in	7½in

Rowan Cotton Glace	2-3 yrs	3-4 yrs	4-5 yrs
A Pink (747 or 799)	1	1	1 x 50g
B Red (741)	1	1	1 x 50g
C Turquoise (809)	1	1	1 x 50g

Small amount of pale green (813) for embroidery.

NEEDLES

1 pair of 3.75mm (US 5) needles.
2mm (US B1) crochet hook.

TENSION

23 sts and 32 rows = 10cm (4in) square measured over stocking stitch using 3.75mm (US 5) needles.

CAP

Using 3.75mm (US 5) needles and yarn A (for alternative colourway, use B for A and A for B), cast on 101 (105: 109) sts and work as follows:

Rows 1 and 2 K to end.
Row 3 (RS) *P1, K1, rep from * to last st, P1.
Row 4 *K1, P1, rep from * to last st, K1.
Rep rows 1 to 4 again, dec 1 st at end of last row on Size 1 only. 100 (105: 109) sts.
Change to st st and start flower chart as follows:
Row 9 K49 (51: 53) B, 2A, 49 (52: 54) B.
Rows 10 to 31 Complete flower from chart.
Using yarn B, cont in st st, starting with a P row, until work meas 13 (14: 15) cm [5 (5½: 6) in], ending with RS facing for next row.

Shape top
Row 1 *K7, K2tog, rep from * to last 1 (6: 1) sts, K1 (6: 1).

Row 2 and alt rows P to end.
Row 3 *K6, K2tog, rep from * to last 1 (6: 1) sts, K1 (6: 1).
Row 5 *K5, K2tog, rep from * to last 1 (6: 1) sts, K1 (6: 1).
Row 7 *K4, K2tog, rep from * to last 1 (6: 1) sts, K1 (6: 1).
Row 9 *K3, K2tog, rep from * to last st, K1.
Row 11 *K2, K2tog, rep from * to last st, K1.
Row 12 *P1, P2tog, rep from * to last st, P1.
Row 13 K2tog across row to last st, K1.
Break yarn, leaving a long loose end for sewing.

EMBROIDERY

Embroider details as indicated on chart.

MAKING UP

Thread yarn through remaining stitches on needle, pull tightly and secure. With RS facing, sew sides together. Weave in any loose ends.

Crochet picot edging

Using 2mm (US B1) crochet hook and yarn C, work a double crochet (US single crochet) and picot edging evenly around bottom of hat as follows:
Picot round (RS) *Work 3dc, make 3 chain and join with a slip stitch in last dc to form picot, rep from *.
Press lightly on WS using a warm iron over a damp cloth, avoiding embroidery.

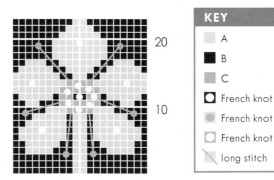

KEY	
☐	A
■	B
▨	C
◻	French knot
●	French knot
◻	French knot
◲	long stitch

STRIPED BEANIE

Be sure to wear this little striped cap with your Big Digger Sweater, as it is a well known scientific fact that hats give you extra brain power!

BEFORE YOU BEGIN

YARN

To fit	2-3 yrs	3-4 yrs	4-5 yrs
Circumference	44cm	46cm	48cm
	17½in	18in	19in
Depth	17cm	18cm	19cm
	6½in	7in	7½in

Rowan Cotton Glace	2-3 yrs	3-4 yrs	4-5 yrs
MC Main colour	1	1	1 x 50g
CC Contrasting colour	1	1	1 x 50g

NEEDLES
1 pair of 3.75mm (US 5) needles.

TENSION
23 sts and 32 rows = 10cm (4in) square measured over stocking stitch using 3.75mm (US 5) needles.

HAT

Using 3.75mm (US 5) needles and yarn MC, cast on 100 (105: 109) sts and work 10 rows in g st (every row, knit). Change to st st and stripe patt of 2 rows yarn CC, 2 rows yarn MC. Cont in patt until work meas 13 (14: 15) cm [5 (5½: 6) in].

Shape top

Row 1 *K7, K2tog, rep from * to last 1 (6: 1) sts, K1 (6: 1).

Row 2 and alt rows P to end.

Row 3 *K6, K2tog, rep from * to last 1 (6: 1) sts, K1 (6: 1).

Row 5 *K5, K2tog, rep from * to last 1 (6: 1) sts, K1 (6: 1).

Row 7 *K4, K2tog, rep from * to last 1 (6: 1) sts, K1 (6: 1).

Row 9 *K3, K2tog, rep from * to last st, K1.

Row 11 *K2, K2tog, rep from * to last st, K1.

Row 12 *P1, P2tog, rep from * to last st, P1.

Row 13 K2tog across row to last st, K1.

Break yarn, leaving a long loose piece for sewing.

MAKING UP

Thread yarn through remaining stitches on needle, pull tightly and secure. With RS facing, sew sides together. Weave in any loose ends. Press lightly on WS using a warm iron over a damp cloth.

BUTTERFLY BAG

This little Butterfly Bag is not only the perfect accessory for the Fantastic Flower Frock, but is very useful for carrying extra sweets and lollipops.

BEFORE YOU BEGIN

YARN

Size	15 x 15cm (6 x 6in)

Rowan Cotton Glace

A Red (741)	1 x 50g
B Pink (747 or 799)	1 x 50g
C Turquoise (809)	1 x 50g

Small amount of pale green (813) for embroidery.

NEEDLES

1 pair of 3.75mm (US 5) needles.
2mm (US B1) crochet hook.

TENSION

23 sts and 32 rows = 10cm (4in) square measured over stocking stitch using 3.75mm (US 5) needles.

GETTING STARTED

BAG

Front
Using 3.75mm (US 5) needles and yarn A, cast on 35 sts and work in patt as follows:
Rows 1 and 2 K to end.
Row 3 (RS) *P1, K1, rep from * to last st, P1.
Row 4 *K1, P1, rep from * to last st, K1.
Rep rows 1 to 4 again. Break yarn A. Change to st st and work rows 1 to 30 from butterfly chart. Change to yarn A and work 8 rows in patt. Cast off.

Back
Using 3.75mm (US 5) needles and yarn A, cast on 35 sts and work 44 rows in patt. Cast off.

Strap
Using 3.75mm (US 5) needles and yarn A, cast on 7 sts and work in patt until strap meas 74cm (29in). Cast off.

EMBROIDERY

Press all pieces lightly on WS using a warm iron over a damp cloth.
Embroider butterfly as indicated on chart.

MAKING UP

With WS facing, pin front and back together.

Picot seam
Using 2mm (US B1) crochet hook and yarn C, starting at top left, join side and bottom seams together with a double crochet (US single crochet) and picot seam as follows:
Picot row (RS) *Work 3dc, make 3 chain and join with a slip stitch in last dc to form picot, rep from *.

Fold strap in half lengthways, WS together, and carefully oversew along length. Sew strap ends securely to inside seam of bag.

KEY	
■	A
□	B
▨	C
◻	French knot
●	French knot
●	French knot
╲	long stich
◣	long stitch
╲	long stitch

BIG DIGGER SWEATER

You can get busy digging around in a sandpit or the garden in this Big Digger Sweater. Dig, dig, dig!

BEFORE YOU BEGIN

YARN

Size	2-3 yrs	3-4 yrs	4-5 yrs
To fit chest	56cm	61cm	66cm
	22in	24in	26in
Actual size	74cm	77.5cm	82.5cm
	29in	30½in	32½in
Back length	37cm	39cm	41cm
	14½in	15½in	16in
Underarm seam	22cm	23cm	24cm
	8½in	9in	9½in

Rowan Cotton Glace	2-3 yrs	3-4 yrs	4-5 yrs
A Navy (746)	3	4	4 x 50g
B Red (741 or 445)	1	1	1 x 50g
C Olive green (814)	1	1	1 x 50g
D Turquoise (809)	1	1	1 x 50g

NEEDLES
1 pair of 3.75mm (US 5) needles.
2 stitch holders.

TENSION
23 sts and 32 rows = 10cm (4in) square measured over stocking stitch using 3.75mm (US 5) needles.

GETTING STARTED

BACK
Using 3.75mm (US 5) needles and yarn A, cast on 85 (89: 95) sts. Work 10 rows in g st (every row, knit).
Row 11 Using yarn A, K to end.
Row 12 Using yarn B,
P to end.
Using yarn A, cont in st st until work meas 21 (22.5: 24) cm [8¼ (9: 9½) in], ending with RS facing for next row.
Change to stripe patt of 2 rows yarn B in st st, 2 rows yarn A in g st. Work 2 rows.

Shape armholes
Keeping stripe patt correct, cast off 2 sts at beg of next 6 rows. 73 (77: 83) sts.
Cont in stripe patt until armhole meas 15 (15.5: 16) cm [5¾ (6: 6¼) in], ending with RS facing for next row.***

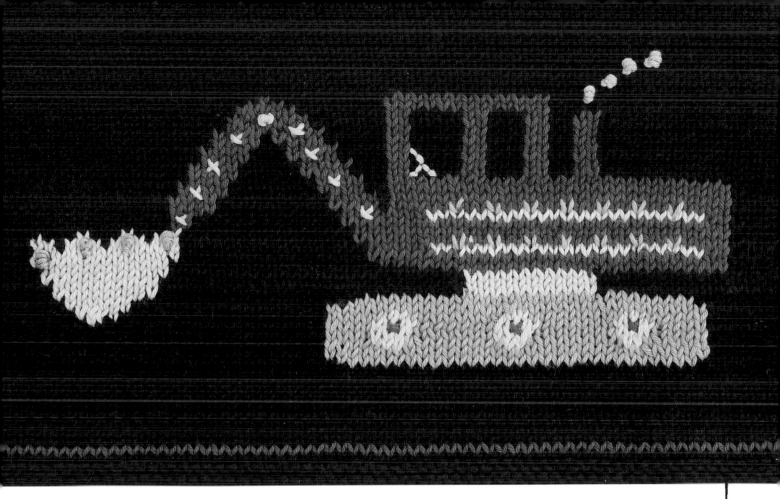

Shape shoulders
Next row Cast off 21 (22: 23) sts, K31 (33: 37),
cast off 21 (22: 23) sts. Break yarns.
Leave 31 (33: 37) sts on holder.

FRONT
Using 3.75mm (US 5) needles and yarn A, cast on
85 (89: 95) sts. Work 10 rows in g st. Change to
st st and, using intarsia method, place digger
chart (see page 59) as follows:
Row 11 K13 (15: 18), work row 11 from digger
chart, K12 (14: 17).
Rows 12 to 57 Cont with chart.
Using yarn A, cont in st st until work meas 21
(22.5: 24) cm [8¼ (9: 9½) in], ending with RS facing
for next row.
Change to stripe patt as on back and work 2 rows.

Shape armholes
Keeping stripe patt correct, cast off 2 sts at beg
of next 6 rows. 73 (77: 83) sts.

Cont in stripe patt until work is 16 (18: 20) rows
*less than back at ***.*

Shape neck
Next row K30 (32: 34), turn and work on
these sts.
Dec 1 st at neck edge on next 5 (6: 7) rows.
Dec 1 st at neck edge on next and foll alt rows
to 21 (22: 23) sts.
Work 3 (4: 5) rows more. Cast off.
Place 13 (13: 15) sts on holder. Rejoin yarn to
rem sts and work to match first side of neck,
reversing all shaping.

SLEEVES
Using 3.75mm (US 5) needles and yarn A, cast on
42 (44: 46) sts and work 10 rows in g st.
Change to st st and inc 1 st at each end of 5th
and every foll 4th row to 68 (72: 76) sts. Cont
without shaping until sleeve meas 22 (23: 24) cm
[8½ (9: 9½) in].

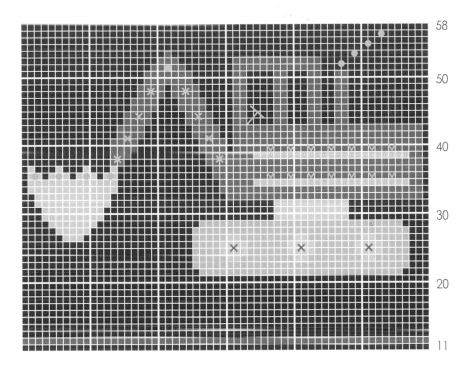

Shape sleevehead

Cast off 2 sts at beg of next 6 rows. Cast off.

EMBROIDERY

Press all pieces lightly on WS using a warm iron over a damp cloth.
Embroider details on front as indicated on chart.

NECKBAND

Join right shoulder seam.

With RS facing and using 3.75mm (US 5) needles and yarn A, pick up and knit 16 (18: 20) sts from left front neck, knit across 13 (13: 15) sts on holder from front neck, pick up and knit 16 (18: 20) sts from right front neck, knit across 31 (33: 37) sts on holder from back neck. Knit 2 rows. Cast off.

MAKING UP

Weave in any loose ends. Join left shoulder seam and neckband. Join side and sleeve seams. Ease sleevehead into armhole and sew into place. Press seams, avoiding embroidery.

BEEP! BEEP! BLANKET

This little blanket is the perfect travelling companion when you set off on your summer holidays.

YARN

Size	102 x 76cm
	40 x 30in

Rowan Cotton Glace

A Navy (746)	6 x 50g
B Turquoise (809)	4 x 50g
C Red (741)	1 x 50g
D Olive green (814)	1 x 50g

NEEDLES

1 pair of long 3.75mm (US 5) needles or circular needle.

TENSION

23 sts and 32 rows = 10cm (4in) square measured over stocking stitch using 3.75mm (US 5) needles.

GETTING STARTED

BLANKET CENTRE

Using 3.75mm (US 5) needles and yarn A, cast on 152 sts and work 24 rows in g st (every row, knit).
Row 25 and 26 Using yarn D, st st.
Row 27 and 28 Using yarn A, K to end.
Row 29 Using yarn A, P to end.
Row 30 Using yarn B, P to end.
Row 31 Using yarn B, K to end.
Rows 32 and 33 Using yarn A, P to end.
Row 34 Using yarn A, K to end.
Rows 35 and 36 Using yarn C, as rows 25 and 26.
Rows 37 to 39 Using yarn A, as rows 27 to 29.
Rows 40 and 41 As rows 30 and 31.
Rows 42 to 44 As rows 32 to 34.
Rows 45 and 46 As rows 25 and 26.
Rows 47 to 57 Using yarn B, st st.
Place car motifs as follows:
Row 58 P10, *work first row of car chart, P18, rep from *, work first row of car chart, P10.

Rows 59 to 80 Complete car motifs.
Rows 81 to 90 Using yarn B, st st.
Rows 91 to 112 As rows 25 to 46.
Rows 113 to 122 Using yarn B, st st.
Place lorry motifs as follows:
Row 123 K5, work first row of lorry chart, K10, work first row of lorry chart, K5.
Rows 124 to 152 Complete lorry motifs.
Rows 153 to 162 Using yarn B, st st.
Rows 163 to 300 Rep rows 25 to 162.
Rows 301 to 322 As rows 25 to 46.
Rows 323 to 346 Using yarn A, K to end.
Cast off.

BLANKET BORDERS

Using 3.75mm (US 5) needles and yarn A, cast on 16 sts and work in g st until border, when slightly stretched, fits length of blanket. Cast off.
Make second piece to match.

EMBROIDERY

Press blanket centre gently on WS using a warm iron over a damp cloth.
Embroider details on cars and lorries as indicated on charts.

MAKING UP

Weave in any loose ends. Pin borders to each long side of blanket and stitch into place.

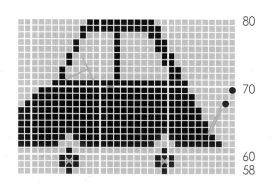

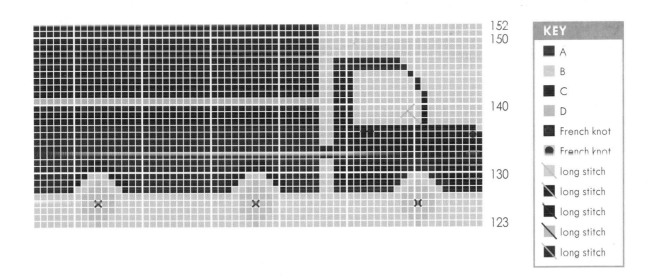

AUTUMN

MOUSIE MOUSIE

Mousie Mousie enjoys eating cheese and skuttling around in skirting boards. Pop her in your pocket and you will have a constant friend.

BEFORE YOU BEGIN

YARN

Height   15cm (6in)

Rowan 4ply Soft
MC Main colour   1 x 50g
A   First contrasting colour   1 x 50g

Small amount of second contrasting colour (B) for embroidery. Washable stuffing.

NEEDLES
1 pair of 3.25mm (US 3) needles.

TENSION
28 sts and 36 rows = 10cm (4in) square measured over stocking stitch using 3.25mm (US 3) needles.

GETTING STARTED

BODY Ⓐ
Using 3.25mm (US 3) needles and yarn MC, cast on 54 sts. Working in st st, follow chart (see page 69), working flowers on chart or working stripes of 2 rows yarn MC, 2 rows yarn A.

BASE Ⓑ
Using 3.25mm (US 3) needles and yarn MC, cast on 4 sts. Working in st st, follow chart.

OUTER EAR Ⓒ
Using 3.25mm (US 3) needles and yarn MC, cast on 16 sts. Working in st st, follow chart.
Make second outer ear.

INNER EAR Ⓓ
Using 3.25mm (US 3) needles and yarn A, cast on 12 sts. Working in st st, follow chart.
Make second inner ear.

TAIL Ⓔ
Using 3.25mm (US 3) needles and yarn A, cast on 4 sts and work 15cm (6in) in st st.

MAKING UP

Press all pieces on WS using a warm iron over a damp cloth. Embroider mouth, eyes and flower centres as indicated on chart.

With RS facing, backstitch body seam. Sew tail to this seam at bottom. Turn RS out and sew base to body, ensuring that shaped decrease edge is at tail end and leaving a gap at tail for stuffing. Stuff mouse evenly, ensuring that stuffing goes into nose. Sew gap.

With WS facing, sew an inner ear to an outer ear and stitch cast-on edges together. Attach securely to body. Repeat for second ear.

Make whiskers using a blunt-ended needle and looping yarn A through nose; secure each loop so that the whiskers cannot be pulled out. Make two loops each side, then cut and trim them.

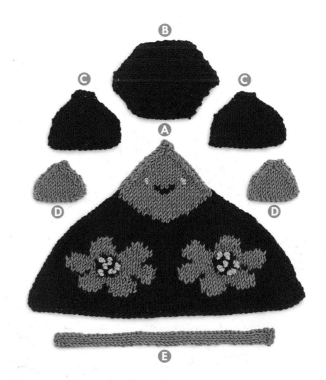

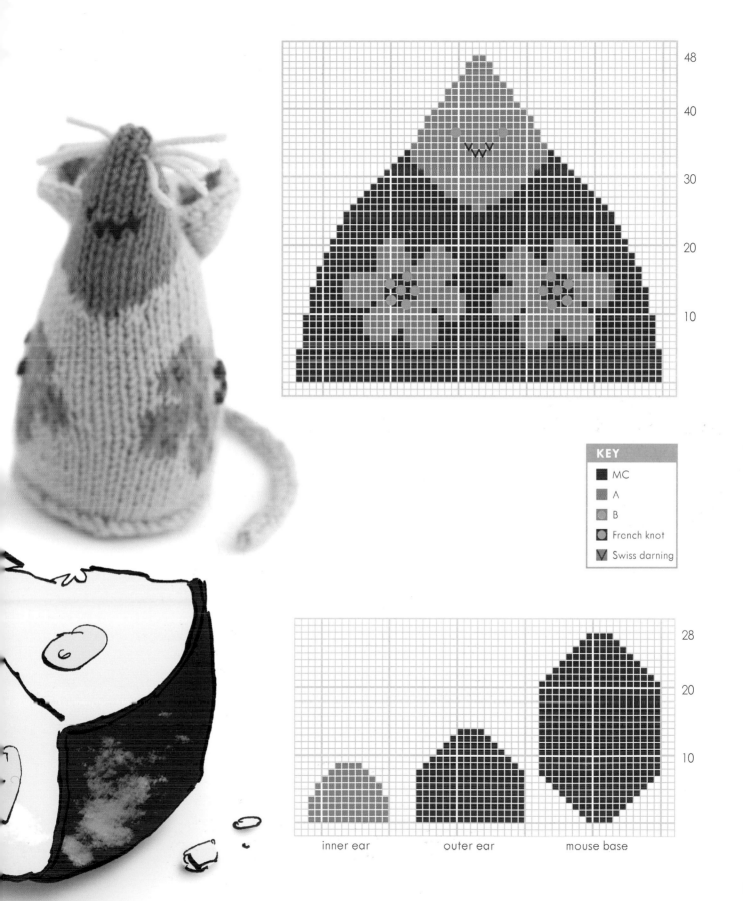

KEY

■ MC
■ A
● B
⬤ French knot
⋁ Swiss darning

inner ear   outer ear   mouse base

WILD FLOWER SWEATER

Bright and cheerful, light and warm, the Wild Flower Sweater is exactly what you need for chilly autumn days.

YARN

Size	2-3 yrs	3-4 yrs	4-5 yrs
To fit chest	56cm	61cm	66cm
	22in	24in	26in
Actual size	69cm	76cm	82cm
	27½in	30in	32½in
Back length	36cm	38cm	40cm
	14in	15in	16in
Sleeve seam	22cm	23cm	24cm
	8½in	9in	9½in

Rowan 4ply Soft	2-3 yrs	3-4 yrs	4-5 yrs
A Turquoise (373)	3	4	4 x 50g
B Red (374)	1	1	1 x 50g
C Pink (377)	1	1	1 x 50g

NEEDLES

1 pair of 3.25mm (US 3) needles.
3mm (US C2) crochet hook.
Cable needle.
Stitch holders.

TENSION

28 sts and 36 rows = 10cm (4in) square measured over stocking stitch using 3.25mm (US 3) needles.

SPECIAL ABBREVIATIONS

c6f = place next 3 sts on cable needle and leave at front of work, K3, K3 from cable needle.
c6b = place next 3 sts on cable needle and leave at back of work, K3, K3 from cable needle.

GETTING STARTED

BACK

Using 3.25mm (US 3) needles and yarn A, cast on 109 (118: 127) sts and work border as follows:
Row 1 K1, *yon, sl1, K1, psso, K4, K2tog, yon, K1, rep from * to end.
Row 2 P2, *K6, P3, rep from * to last 8 sts, K6, P2.

Row 3 K2, *yon, sl1, K1, psso, K2, K2tog, yon, K3, rep from * to last 8 sts, yon, sl1, K1, psso, K2, K2tog, yon, K2.
Row 4 P3, *K4, P5, rep from * to last 7 sts, K4, P3.
Row 5 K3, *yon, sl1, K1, psso, K2tog, yon, K5, rep from * to last 7 sts, yon, sl1, K1, psso, K2tog, yon, K3.
Row 6 P4, *K2, P7, rep from * to last 6 sts, K2, P4.
Rows 7 to 12 As rows 1 to 6.
Change to st st and work 2 rows.
Place flower panel chart (see page 75) as follows:
Row 3 K10 (14: 19), work row 1 of flower panel chart, K9 (14: 18).
Rows 4 to 71 Cont with flower panel chart, dec 1 st at each end of row 11 and 6 foll 10th rows. 97 (106: 115) sts.
Work 5 (9: 13) rows in st st.

Shape armholes

Cast off 2 sts at beg of next 6 rows. 85 (94: 103) sts.
Work 4 rows in st st, dec 1 st at end of last row on Size 2 only. 85 (93: 103) sts.

Start cable detail

Row 1 K27 (31: 36), *(P1, K1) 3 times, K7, rep from * twice more, K to end.
Row 2 P26 (30: 35), *(K1, P1) 4 times, P5, rep from * twice more, P to end.
Rows 3 and 4 As rows 1 and 2.
Row 5 K23 (27: 32), (c6f, K1, c6b) 3 times, K to end.
Rows 6 to 12 St st.
Row 13 K23 (27: 32), (c6b, K1, c6f) 3 times, K to end.
Row 14 As row 2.
Rows 15 to 18 As rows 1 to 2, twice.**
Work 26 (28: 30) rows in st st.

Shape neck
Row 1 K25 (28: 31),
cast off 35 (37: 41) sts,
K25 (28: 31).
Row 2 P to end.
Row 3 Cast off 5 sts,
work to end.
Cast off.
With WS facing, rejoin
yarn to rem sts at neck
edge and work to match first
side, reversing all shaping.

FRONT

Work as for back to **
(completion of cable detail).
Work 10 (12: 12) rows in st st.

Shape neck
Row 1 K32 (36: 41),
cast off 21 sts, K32
(36: 41).
Row 2 P to end.
Row 3 Cast off 3
(4: 5) sts, K to end.

Rows 4 to 8 Dec 1 st at neck edge.

Rows 9 to 16 Dec 1 st at neck edge on alt rows. 20 (23: 27) sts.

Size 3, dec 1 st at neck edge on foll alt row. 26 sts.

All sizes, work 2 rows in st st. Cast off.

Rejoin yarn to rem sts and work to match first side of neck, reversing all shaping.

SLEEVES

Using 3.25mm (US 3) needles and yarn A, cast on 55 (55: 64) sts and work 12 rows in border patt as for back.

Change to st st, inc 1 st at each end of 3rd and every foll 10th row to 67 (67: 74) sts. Cont without shaping until sleeve meas 22 (23: 24) cm [8½ (9: 9½) in].

Shape sleevehead

Cast off 2 sts at beg of next 6 rows. Cast off.

EMBROIDERY

Press all pieces lightly on WS using a warm iron over a damp cloth. Embroider details on back and front as indicated on chart.

NECKBAND

Join right shoulder seam. Using 3mm (US C2) crochet hook and B, work 1 row of double crochet (US single crochet) around neck.

MAKING UP

Weave in any loose ends. Join left shoulder seam. Join side and sleeve seams. Ease sleevehead into armhole and sew into place. Press seams, avoiding embroidery.

KEY	
▨	A
■	B
▨	C
◉	French knot
●	French knot
●	French knot
◣	long stitch

DOUGIE DOG SWEATER

Warm and woolly Dougie Dog Sweater is just the thing for a walk in the woods. You can keep autumn leaves and conkers in the pocket.

YARN

Size	2-3 yrs	3-4 yrs	4-5 yrs
To fit chest	56cm	61cm	66cm
	22in	24in	26in
Actual size	75cm	79cm	83cm
	29½in	31in	33in
Back length	37cm	39cm	41cm
	14½in	15½in	16in
Underarm seam	22cm	23cm	24cm
	8½in	9in	9½in

Rowan 4ply Soft	2-3 yrs	3-4 yrs	4-5 yrs
A Red (374)	5	5	6 x 50g
B Turquoise (373)	1	1	1 x 50g
C Dark brown (389)	1	1	1 x 50g
D Off-white (376)	1	1	1 x 50g

NEEDLES

1 pair of 3.25mm (US 3) needles.
Stitch holders.
Cable needle.
2mm (US B1) crochet hook.

TENSION

30 sts and 36 rows = 10cm (4in) square measured, after pressing, over textured patt using 3.25mm (US 3) needles.

SPECIAL ABBREVIATION

c2R = knit the 2nd stitch, then knit the first stitch.

BACK

Using 3.25mm (US 3) needles and yarn A, cast on 112 (118: 124) sts and work textured patt as follows:
Row 1 *P1, K2, rep from * to last st, P1.
Row 2 *K1, P2, rep from * to last st, K1.
Rows 3 and 4 As rows 1 and 2.
Row 5 *P1, c2R, rep from * to last st, P1.

Rows 2 to 5 form patt rep. Cont in patt until work meas 22 (23.5: 25) cm [8¾ (9½: 9¾) in], ending with RS facing for next row.

Shape armholes

Cast off 3 sts at beg of next 6 rows. 94 (100: 106) sts.
Cont in patt until armhole meas 15 (15.5: 16) cm [5¾ (6: 6¼) in], ending with RS facing for next row.

Shape shoulders

Cast off 10 (11: 12) sts at beg of next 4 rows.
Leave 54 (56: 58) sts on holder.

FRONT

Work as for back until work meas 28 (30: 32) cm [11 (11¾: 12½) in], ending with RS facing for next row.

Shape neck

Next row Patt 35 (37: 39), turn.
Dec 1 st at neck edge on next 8 rows. Dec 1 st at neck edge on foll 7 alt rows. 20 (22: 24) sts.
Cont in patt until work meas same as back at shoulder, ending with RS facing for next row.

Shape shoulder

Next row Cast off 10 (11: 12) sts, patt to end.
Work 1 row. Cast off.
Place centre 24 (26: 28) sts on stitch holder. With RS facing, rejoin yarn to rem sts and work to match first side of neck, reversing all shaping.

SLEEVES

Using 3.25mm (US 3) needles and yarn A, cast on 61 (64: 67) sts. Working in textured patt as for back, inc 1 st at each end of 9th and every foll 4th row to 91 (96: 101) sts, working extra sts into patt. Cont without shaping until sleeve meas 22 (23: 24) cm [8½ (9: 9½) in].

Shape sleevehead

Cast off 3 sts at beg of next 6 rows. Cast off.

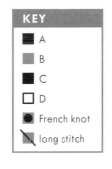
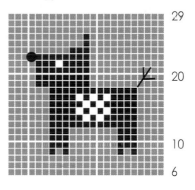

29
20
10
6

POCKET

Using 3.25mm (US 3) needles and yarn A, cast on 31 sts and work 5 rows in textured patt.

Row 6 Using yarn A, patt 4; using yarn B purl across row 6 of dog chart; using yarn A, patt 4.

Rows 7 to 29 Work from dog chart in st st with 4 sts in patt in yarn A each side.

Row 30 Using yarn A, patt 4, K23, patt 4. Work 6 rows more in patt. Cast off.

NECKBAND

Join right shoulder seam.

Using 3.25mm (US 3) needles and yarn A, pick up and knit 26 (27: 28) sts down left side of front neck, patt across 24 (26: 28) sts on holder, pick up and knit 26 (27: 28) sts up right side front neck, patt across back neck sts. Starting with row 4, work 7 rows in patt. Cast off in patt.

EMBROIDERY

Press pocket lightly on WS using a warm iron over a damp cloth. Embroider details as indicated on chart.

MAKING UP

Weave in any loose ends. Press all pieces lightly on WS using a warm iron over a damp cloth. Join left shoulder seam and neckband. Join side and sleeve seams. Ease sleevehead into armhole and sew into place. Stitch pocket into position as shown.

DOUGIE DOG HAT & SCARF

Essential woolly warmth for outdoor activities on blustery days and starry cold nights. Wrap up!

BEFORE YOU BEGIN

YARN

Hat, to fit	2-3 yrs	3-4 yrs	4-5 yrs
Circumference	46cm	47cm	48cm
	18in	18½in	19in
Depth	18cm	19cm	20cm
	7in	7½in	8in

Scarf, one size

Rowan 4ply Soft	2-3 yrs	3-4 yrs	4-5 yrs
A Red (374)	1	1	1 x 50g
B Turquoise (373)	3	3	3 x 50g
C Dark brown (389)	1	1	1 x 50g
Small amount of off-white (376) for embroidery.			

NEEDLES
1 pair of 3.25mm (US 3) needles.
2mm (US B1) crochet hook.

TENSION
30 sts and 36 rows = 10cm (4in) square measured, after pressing, over textured patt using 3.25mm (US 3) needles.

SPECIAL ABBREVIATION
c2R = knit the 2nd st, then knit the first st.

HAT

Using 3.25mm (US 3) needles and yarn A, cast on 139 (142: 145) sts and work 13 rows in textured patt as follows:

Row 1 *P1, K2, rep from * to last st, P1.
Row 2 *K1, P2, rep from * to last st, K1.
Rows 3 and 4 As rows 1 and 2.
Row 5 *P1, c2R, rep from * to last st, P1.
Rows 2 to 5 form patt rep.
Rows 6 to 13 Patt.
Change to st st and, starting with a WS row, work rows 14 to 38 from dog chart. Using yarn B, change to textured patt, starting with a patt row 1, and cont until work meas 18 (19: 20) cm [7 (7½: 8) in]. Cast off.

TIE

Using 2mm (US B1) crochet hook and yarn B, make a length of chain stitches about 50cm (20in) long, leaving long loose ends at each end for attaching tassels.

TASSEL (MAKE 2)

Cut a piece of thick card to 6cm (2½in) deep. Wrap yarn B around it 10 times and, using a large blunt-ended needle, slip a separate strand of yarn through top and knot it. Carefully slip tassel from card and knot a double length of yarn around tassel about 1cm (½in) from knotted top, then pass tie yarn through tassel and down to bottom so that it becomes part of tassel. Cut bottom loops and trim.

MAKING UP

Weave in any loose ends. Press hat to size using a warm iron over a damp cloth. Work embroidery details (dogs noses and tails) as indicated on chart. Join side seam (this seam now becomes centre back of hat). Join top seam. Pass tie through top corner of both seams and attach tassels. Pull two corners together and tie tassels in a bow (see page 81).

SCARF

Using 3.25mm (US 3) needles and yarn A, cast on 100 sts and work 13 rows in textured patt as for hat.

Work from ** to ** as for hat, then cont in patt until work measures 116cm (46in), ending with RS facing for next row. Work dog panel again BUT start with row 38 and work to row 14 (so turning dogs upside down).
Change to yarn A and purl 1 row. Work 13 rows in textured patt. Cast off in patt.

MAKING UP

Weave in any loose ends. Press scarf using a warm iron over a damp cloth. Work embroidery details as indicated on chart.
With WS together, sew together row-end edges and end seams, working end seams so that long seam runs down centre back of scarf, and leaving a 10cm (4in) gap at centre back neck. Turn scarf RS out through gap and stitch gap closed.

KEY

- ■ A
- ▨ B
- ■ C
- ☐ D
- ● French knot
- ＼ long stitch

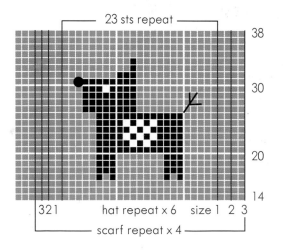

23 sts repeat

38
30
20
14

3 2 1   hat repeat x 6   size 1 2 3
scarf repeat x 4

MY HOUSE BLANKET

My House Blanket makes the perfect extra layer on your bed as autumn nights get chillier. Snuggle under and cosy up!

BEFORE YOU BEGIN

YARN

Size	114 x 140cm
	45 x 55in

Rowan 4ply Soft

Turquoise (373)	13 x 50g

NEEDLES

1 pair of long 3.25mm (US 3) needles or 3.25mm (US 3) circular needle.

TENSION

28 sts and 36 rows = 10cm (4in) square measured over stocking stitch using 3.25mm (US 3) needles.

GETTING STARTED

BLANKET

Using 3.25mm (US 3) needles, cast on 284 sts and work 16 rows in g st (every row, knit), dec 1 st at each end of alt rows. 268 sts.

Cont as follows:

Row 1 (RS) P to end.

Rows 2 and 3 K to end.

Row 4 P to end.

Row 5 K to end.

Row 6 P to end.

Place border trees (chart 1, page 86) as follows:

Row 7 K12, P10 (tree, chart 1), K49, P10 (tree), K48, P10 (tree), K48, P10 (tree), K49, P10 (tree), K12.

Rows 8 to 47 Complete trees from chart 1, following chart rows 2 to 41, working trees in rev st st and background in st st, and making bobbles as follows:

Bobble on RS rows (K1, P1, K1) into st, turn, P3, turn, K3, turn, P3, turn, sl1, K1, psso.

Bobble on WS rows (P1, K1, P1) into st, turn, K3, turn, P3, turn, K3, turn, P3tog.

Rows 48 to 51 St st, starting with a P row.

Row 52 P34, K200, P34.

Row 53 K34, P200, K34.

Row 54 P34, K200, P34.

Row 55 K to end.

Row 56 P to end.

Row 57 K34, *P2, K2, rep from * to last 34 sts, K34.

Row 58 P to end.

Row 59 K to end.

Rows 60 to 67 As rows 52 to 59.

Rows 68 to 70 As rows 52 to 54.

Rows 71 to 74 St st, starting with a K row.

Place houses and trees as follows:

Row 75 K46, P10 (tree, chart 1), K10, P45 (house, chart 2), K18, P10 (tree), K18, P45 (house, chart 3), K10, P10 (tree), K46.

Rows 76 to 115 Work rev st st trees and houses from charts with st st background.

Rows 116 to 133 Cont with houses.

Place edge trees as follows:

Row 134 P12, K10 (tree, chart 1), patt to last 22 sts, K10 (tree), P12.

Rows 135 to 166 Cont with edge trees and houses.

Rows 167 to 170 Cont with edge trees.

Row 171 Patt 34, P200, patt 34.

Row 172 Patt 34, K200, patt 34.

Row 173 As row 171.

Row 174 As row 171 (finish edge trees).

Row 175 K to end.

Row 176 P34, *K2, P2, rep from * to last 34 sts, P34.

Rows 177 and 178 St st, starting with a K row.

Row 179 K34, P200, K34.

Row 180 P34, K200, P34.

Row 181 K34, P200, K34.

Rows 182 and 183 St st, starting with a P row.

Row 184 As row 176.

chart 1

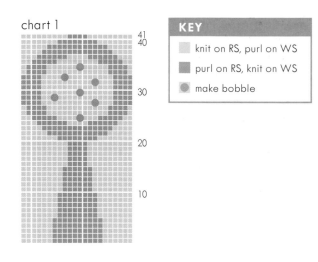

41
40

30

20

10

Rows 185 and 186 St st, starting with a K row.

Rows 187 to 189 As rows 179 to 181.

Rows 190 to 193 St st, starting with a P row.

Place houses and trees as follows:

Row 194 P46, K10 (tree), P10, K45 (house, chart 5), P18, K10 (tree), P18, K45 (house, chart 4), P10, K10 (tree), P46.

Rows 195 to 234 Cont with houses and trees.

Rows 235 to 252 Cont with houses.

Place edge trees as follows:

Row 253 K12, P10 (tree), patt to last 22 sts, P10 (tree), K12.

Rows 254 to 285 Cont with houses and edge trees.

chart 2

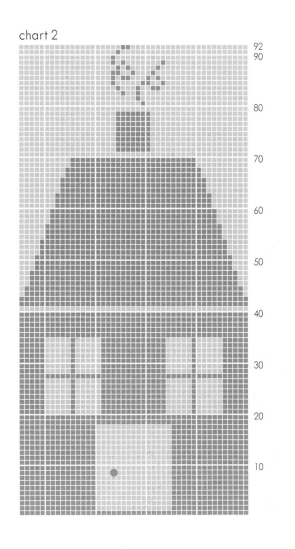

92
90

80

70

60

50

40

30

20

10

chart 3

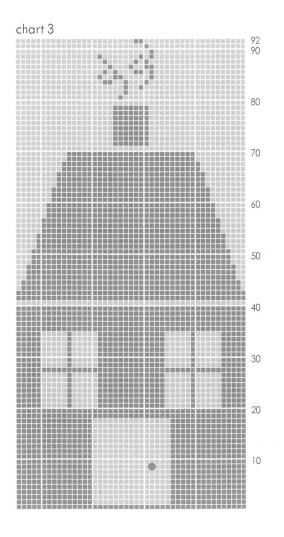

92
90

80

70

60

50

40

30

20

10

Rows 286 to 289 Cont with edge trees.

Row 290 Patt 34, K200, patt 34.

Row 291 Patt 34, P200, patt 34.

Row 292 As row 290.

Row 293 As row 290.

Row 294 P to end.

Rows 295 to 308 As rows 57 to 70.

Rows 309 to 431 As rows 71 to 193.

Place border trees as follows:

Row 432 P12, K10 (tree), P49, K10 (tree), P48, K10 (tree), P48, K10 (tree), P49, K10 (tree), P12.

Rows 433 to 471 Cont with border trees.

Rows 472 to 474 St st, starting with a P row.

Rows 475 and 476 K to end.

Row 477 P to end.

Row 478 K to end.

Rows 479 to 494 K to end, inc 1 st at each end of alt rows. 284 sts. Cast off loosely.

EDGING

Using 3.25mm (US 3) needles, pick up 372 sts along straight side of blanket. Work 16 rows in g st (every row, knit), inc 1 st at each end of alt rows. Cast off loosely. Rep for other side.

MAKING UP

Weave in any loose ends. Join mitred corners. Press lightly using a warm iron over a damp cloth, avoiding bobbles.

chart 4

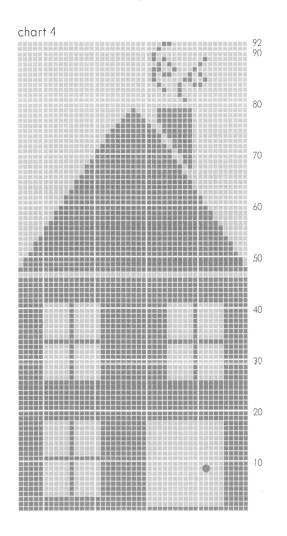

chart 5

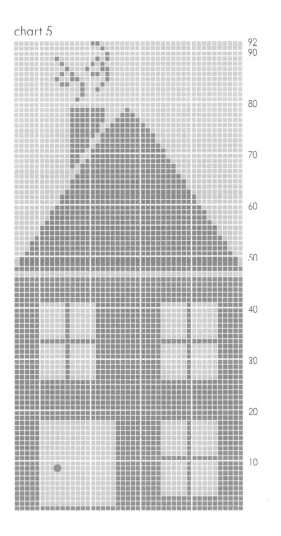

MONSIEUR CAT

Monsieur Cat naturally prefers cream to milk and can spend hours happily sat with you in front of a cosy open fire.

BEFORE YOU BEGIN

YARN
Height   22cm (8½in)

Rowan Kid Classic
A Terracotta (827)   1 x 50g
B Off-white (828)   1 x 50g

Washable stuffing.

NEEDLES
1 pair of 5.5mm (US 9) needles.

TENSION
18 sts and 23 rows = 10cm (4in) square measured over stocking stitch using 5.5mm (US 9) needles.

GETTING STARTED

BACK Ⓐ
Using 5.5mm (US 9) needles and yarn A, cast on 33 sts and work in alternating st st stripes of 2 rows yarn A and 2 rows yarn B as follows:

Row 1 (Yarn A), K to end.
Row 2 Cast on 2 sts, P to last st, inc.
Row 3 (Yarn B), cast on 2 sts, K to last st, inc.
Row 4 As row 2.
Row 5 (Yarn A), as row 3.
Row 6 Cast on 1 st, P to last st, inc. 47 sts.
Row 7 (Yarn B), K to end.
Row 8 P1, P2tog tbl, P to last 3 sts, P2tog, P1.
Rows 9 to 36 Keeping stripe sequence correct, as rows 7 and 8, 14 times.
Row 37 K1, K2tog, K to last 3 sts, sl1, K1, psso, K1.
Row 38 As row 8.
Rows 39 to 42 As rows 37 and 38, twice. 5 sts. Cast off.

FRONT Ⓑ
Using 5.5mm (US 9) needles and yarn A, cast on 23 sts. Working in st st, follow chart (see page 95) and work decreases on knit and purl rows as follows:

Dec on a knit row K1, K2tog, K to last 3 sts, sl1, K1, psso, K1.
Dec on a purl row P1, P2tog tbl, P to last 3 sts, P2tog, P1.
When knitting nose, leave long loose ends of yarn to use to embroider mouth and whiskers.

BASE Ⓒ
Using 5.5mm (US 9) needles and yarn A, cast on 17 sts and work as follows:

Row 1 K to end.
Row 2 Cast on 2 sts, P to last st, inc.
Row 3 Cast on 2 sts, K to last st, inc.
Rows 4 to 6 St st.
Row 7 K1, sl1, K1, psso, K to last 3 sts, K2tog, K1.
Row 8 P to end.
Rep rows 7 and 8 until 5 sts rem. Cast off.

TAIL Ⓓ
Work in stripe patt as for back, working last 4 rows in yarn A.
Using 5.5mm (US 9) needles and yarn A, cast on 8 sts and work 27 rows in stripe patt.

Row 28 P1, P2tog, P to last 3 sts, P2tog tbl, P1.
Row 29 K to end.
Rows 30 and 31 As rows 28 and 29.
Row 32 P2tog twice.
Row 33 K2tog. Fasten off.
Make a second tail piece.

OUTER EAR Ⓔ
Using 5.5mm (US 9) needles and yarn A, cast on 9 sts and work as follows:

Rows 1 and 2 St st.
Row 3 K1, sl1, K1, psso, K to last 3 sts, K2tog, K1.
Row 4 P to end.
Rows 5 and 6 As rows 3 and 4.
Row 7 K1, sl1, K2tog, psso, K1.

Row 8 P3tog. Fasten off.
Make second outer ear.

INNER EAR  **F**
Using 5.5mm (US 9) needles and yarn A, cast on 7 sts and work as follows:
Rows 1 and 2 St st.

Row 3 K1, sl1, K1, psso, K to last 3 sts, K2tog, K1.
Row 4 P to end.
Row 5 K1, sl1, K2tog, psso, K1.
Row 6 P to end.
Row 7 K3tog. Fasten off.
Make second inner ear.

MAKING UP

Press all pieces very lightly on WS using a warm iron over a damp cloth.

Using long loose ends of A left when knitting nose, make loops of yarn secured to nose area for whiskers. Cut loops evenly to obtain whiskers. Embroider mouth and make French knots for eyes as indicated on chart. Fasten all ends neatly, ensuring that no waste yarn can be seen through knitting.

Use backstitch to sew all seams. With RS facing, sew straight seam of base to cast-on edge of front, and side seams of back to front.

With RS facing, sew along tail, leaving cast-on edge open for stuffing. Turn RS out. With RS facing, sew one side of tail cast-on edge to smallest edge of base. Stuff tail to a uniform thickness of 3cm (1¼in).

With RS facing, sew together back and base seam, ensuring that tail is securely stitched to back and leaving an opening of 2.5cm (1in). Turn RS out and carefully stuff Monseur Cat, making sure he has a good shape. Sew gap.

With WS facing, sew together an outer ear with an inner ear, then stitch into position on Monsieur Cat. Repeat for second ear.

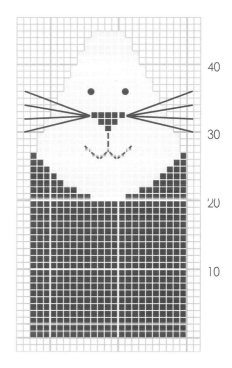

40

30

20

10

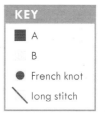

KEY

■ A

□ B

● French knot

╱ long stitch

JACK FROST JACKET

Keep Jack Frost's nip away when you are out and about in this wonderfully warm and sumptuously soft jacket.

YARN

Size	2-3 yrs	3-4 yrs	4-5 yrs
To fit chest	56cm	61cm	66cm
	22in	24in	26in
Actual chest	66cm	72cm	76cm
	26in	28½in	30in
Back length	40cm	42cm	44cm
	16in	16½in	17½in
Underarm seam	22cm	24cm	26cm
	8½in	9½in	10in

Rowan Kid Classic	2-3 yrs	3-4 yrs	4-5 yrs
A Red (847)	3	3	3 x 50g
B Pink (819)	2	3	3 x 50g
C Off-white (828)	1	1	1 x 50g

Small amount of terracotta (827) for embroidery.

NEEDLES

1 pair of 5.5mm (US 9) needles.
2mm (US B1) and 4mm (US G6) crochet hooks.

TENSION

18 sts and 23 rows = 10cm (4in) square measured over stocking stitch using 5.5mm (US 9) needles.
18 sts and 28 rows = 10cm (4in) square measured over textured stitch using 5.5mm (US 9) needles.

GETTING STARTED

BACK

Using 5.5mm (US 9) needles and yarn A, cast on 122 (132: 142) sts and work border as follows:
Row 1 K1, *yon, K5, lift 2nd, 3rd, 4th and 5th sts over the first st, rep from * to last st, yon, K1.
Row 2 K1, *(P1, yon, K1 tbl) into next st, P1, rep from * to end.
Row 3 K2tog, K1 tbl, *K3, K1 tbl, rep from * to last 2 sts, K2tog. 99 (107: 115) sts.
Row 4 to 50 Change to yarn B and st st, starting with a P row, and follow chart for back. Change to yarn A and textured stitch as follows:

Row 1 K1, sl1 purlwise, *K3, sl1 purlwise, rep from * to last st, K1.
Row 2 P1, sl1 purlwise, *P3, sl1 purlwise, rep from * to last st, P1.
Row 3 *K3, sl1 purlwise, rep from * to last 3 sts, K3.
Row 4 *P3, sl1 purlwise, rep from * to last 3 sts, P3.
Rows 1 to 4 form patt rep. Cont in patt until work meas 25 (27: 28) cm [10 (10½: 11¼) in], ending with RS facing for next row.

Shape armholes

Cast off 4 (6: 8) sts at beg of next 2 rows.
Cont in patt until armhole meas 15 (15: 16) cm [6 (6: 6¼) in], ending with RS facing for next row.

Shape shoulders and neck

Row 1 Patt 21 (22: 23) sts, cast off 29 (31: 33) sts, patt 21 (22: 23) sts.
Work on 21 (22: 23) sts as follows:
Row 2 Patt.
Row 3 Dec 1 st at neck edge, patt to end.
Row 4 Patt.
Cast off. With WS facing, rejoin yarn to rem sts at neck edge and work to match first side.

LEFT FRONT

Using 5.5mm (US 9) needles and yarn A, cast on 62 (67: 72) sts and work 2 rows of border as on back.
Row 3 K2tog, K1 tbl, K2tog, K1, K1 tbl, *K3, K1 tbl, rep from * to last 6 sts, K2tog, K1, K1 tbl, K2tog. 49 (53: 57) sts.
Row 4 to 50 Change to yarn B and st st, starting with a purl row, and follow chart for left front.
Change to yarn A and textured stitch as on back. Cont until work meas 25 (27: 28) cm [10 (10½: 11¼) in], ending with RS facing for next row.

Shape armhole

Cast off 4 (6: 8) sts, patt to end.
Work 3 rows more.

Shape neck

Dec 1 st at neck edge on next and every foll alt row until 23 (24: 25) sts rem. Work 1 row.
Dec 1 st at neck edge on next and every foll 4th row until 20 (21: 22) sts rem.
Cont without shaping until work meas same as back at shoulder. Cast off.

RIGHT FRONT

Work to match left front, reversing all shaping and working an extra row before armhole.

SLEEVES

Using 5.5mm (US 9) needles and yarn A, cast on 37 (37: 42) sts and work 2 rows of border as on back.
Row 3 K2, K1 tbl, *K3, K1 tbl, rep from * to last 2 sts, K2. 33 (33: 37) sts.
Row 4 Inc, P to last 2 sts, inc, P1.
Change to textured st as on back. Inc 1 st at each end of every foll 3rd row to 73 (75: 77) sts, working extra sts into patt. Work 3 (4: 11) rows without shaping, ending with

RS facing for next row. Sleeve should meas 22 (24: 26) cm [8½ (9½: 10) in].

Shape sleevehead

Cast off 2 sts beg of next 6 rows. Cast off.

EMBROIDERY

Press all pieces very lightly on WS using a warm iron over a damp cloth. Embroider French knots as indicated on charts.

MAKING UP

Weave in any loose ends. Join shoulder, side and underarm seams. Ease sleevehead into armhole and stitch.

Crochet buttons

Using 2mm (US B1) crochet hook and yarn A, work a double crochet (US single crochet) button as follows:

Make 3 chain and join with a slip stitch in first chain to form a ring.

Round 1 6dc into ring.

Round 2 *1dc into each of next 2dc, 2dc into next dc, rep from * once more. 8dc.

Round 3 *Draw a loop through each of next 2dc, draw a loop through all 3 loops on hook, rep from * 3 times more. 4dc.

Fasten off, leaving a long loose end. Weave loose end through edge, pull to gather, and secure. Repeat for second button.

Crochet edging

Using 4mm (US G6) crochet hook and yarn A, work 1 row of double crochet (US single crochet) up right front, across back neck and down left front, turn and work double crochet back making 2 loops of 5 chain stitches for each of two buttonholes on right front (see page 97). Sew on buttons.

KEY	
▨	B
▨	C
●	French knot
●	French knot

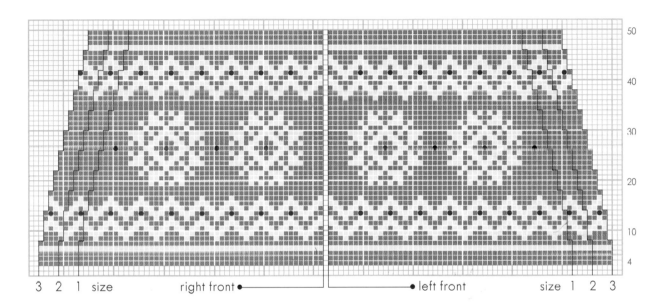

3　2　1　size　　　　　right front ●—————————● left front　　　　　size　1　2　3

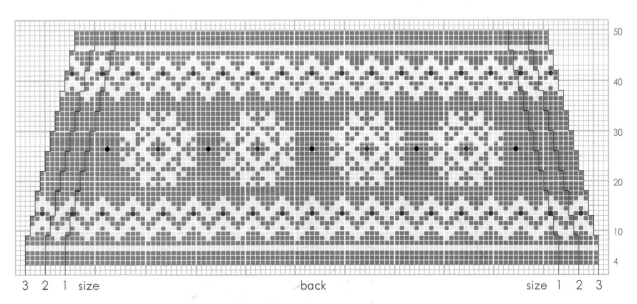

3　2　1　size　　　　　　　　　back　　　　　　　　　size　1　2　3

WOOLLY CAP & SCARF

Woolly Cap and Scarf are ideal snowballing companions with the Jack Frost Jacket. Do you think Arctic rabbits feel this warm?

YARN

Hat, to fit	2-3 yrs	3-4 yrs	4-5 yrs
Circumference	44cm	46cm	48cm
	17½in	18in	19in
Depth	17cm	18cm	19cm
	6½in	7in	7½in

Scarf, one size.

Rowan Kid Classic
Pink (819) or red (847)   2 x 50g for hat and scarf

NEEDLES

1 pair of 5.5mm (US 9) needles.

TENSION

18 sts and 23 rows = 10cm (4in) square measured over stocking stitch using 5.5mm (US 9) needles.

GETTING STARTED

CAP

Using 5.5mm (US 9) needles, cast on 97 (102: 107) sts and work edging as follows:

Row 1 K1, *yon, K5, lift 2nd, 3rd, 4th and 5th sts over the first st, rep from * to last st, yon, K1.

Row 2 P1, *(P1, yon, K1 tbl) into next st, P1, rep from * to end.

Row 3 K2, K1 tbl, *K3, K1 tbl, rep from * to last 2 sts, K2.

Row 4 P2tog, P to end. 80 (84: 88) sts.

Work 18 (20: 22) rows in st st.

Shape top

Work Size 2 (3-4 yrs) only as follows:

Row 1 *K19, K2tog, rep from * to end.

Row 2 P to end. 80 sts.

Work Size 3 (4-5 yrs) only as follows:

Row 1 Inc, K to last st, inc.

Row 2 P to end. 90 sts.

Work all sizes as follows:

Row 1 *K8, K2tog, rep from * to end.

Row 2 and alt rows P to end.

Row 3 *K7, K2tog, rep from * to end.

Row 5 *K6, K2tog, rep from * to end.

Cont dec on knit rows, working 1 st less between decreases until 16 (16: 18) sts rem.

Next row P2tog across row.

Break yarn, leaving a long loose end for sewing.

MAKING UP

Thread yarn through remaining stitches on needle, pull tightly and secure. With RS facing, sew sides together. Weave in any loose ends. Press very lightly on WS using a warm iron over a damp cloth.

SCARF

Using 5.5mm (US 9) needles, cast on 42 sts. Work 4 rows of edging as for hat. 36 sts.

Rows 5 to 14 Work in st st.

Row 15 K2, s1, K1, psso, K to last 4 sts, K2tog, K2.

Cont in st st, dec as row 15 on rows 23, 31, 37, 43 and 49. 24 sts.

Work 25 rows more in st st. Cast off.

Make 3 more pieces in same way.

MAKING UP

With RS facing, sew two pieces together at cast-off edge (this makes one side of scarf). Rep for other two pieces. Press lightly on WS using a warm iron over a damp cloth. With RS of scarf together, join side seams using backstitch. Turn RS out and sew both ends with a running stitch along wavy edge of border.

If desired, make two-flower posy to go with scarf using a contrasting Rowan Kid Classic colour for flowers (see page 28).

COSY SOCKS

These cosy socks are so soft and so gentle on your skin and they are just what you need to slip on after a bedtime bath. There's lots of room for your toes to relax in them!

BEFORE YOU BEGIN

YARN

To fit	2-3 yrs	3-4 yrs	4-5 yrs
Foot length	14cm	16cm	18cm
	5½in	6½in	7in

Rowan Kid Classic	2-3 yrs	3-4 yrs	4-5 yrs
MC Main colour	1	1	1 x 50g
CC Contrasting colour	1	1	1 x 50g

NEEDLES

1 pair each of 4mm (US 6) and 5mm (US 8) needles.
Stitch holders.

TENSION

18 sts and 23 rows = 10cm (4in) square measured over stocking stitch using 5mm (US 8) needles.

GETTING STARTED

SOCKS

Using 5mm (US 8) needles and yarn CC, cast on 40 sts and work as follows:

Rows 1 and 2 *K2, P2, rep from * to end.
Rows 3 and 4 Using MC, work as rows 1 and 2.
Rows 1 to 4 form striped rib patt. Work 2 rows more in patt.
Change to 4mm (US 6) needles and cont in patt to completion of row 22.

Change to 5mm (US 8) needles and work 2 rows in yarn MC, then 2 rows in yarn CC. Break yarns.

Divide for foot
Next row Slip first 10 sts onto a stitch holder, then using B, K20, slip last 10 sts onto a stitch holder.
Working on these 20 sts and using MC, work 19 (21: 23) rows more in st st.

Shape toe
Row 1 K2, s1, K1, psso, K to last 4 sts, K2tog, K2.
Row 2 P2, P2tog, P to last 4 sts, P2tog tbl, P2.
Rep rows 1 and 2 until 8 sts rem.
Next row K2tog across row.
Cast off.
Slip the 2 sets of 10 sts onto 5mm (US 8) needle (edges to centre on needle). With RS facing and using yarn CC, work 10 rows in st st.

Shape heel
Row 1 K11, K2tog tbl, K1, turn.
Row 2 Sl1, P3, P2tog, P1, turn.
Row 3 Sl1, K4, K2tog tbl, K1, turn.
Row 4 Sl1, P5, P2tog, P1, turn.
Cont working 1 st more before dec on each row until all 12 sts are on one needle. Break yarn CC.
Next row With RS facing and using yarn MC, pick up and knit 10 sts from side of heel, K12 from needle and pick up and knit 10 sts from other side of heel. 32 sts.
Next row P to end.

Shape instep
Row 1 K2, sl1, K1, psso, K to last 4 sts, K2tog, K2.
Row 2 P to end.
Rep rows 1 and 2 until 20 sts rem.
Work 6 (8: 10) rows in st st.
Shape toe as before. Cast off.

MAKING UP

Weave in any loose ends. Join foot and leg seams.
Press very lightly on WS using a warm iron over a damp cloth.

FIRESIDE BLANKET

The Fireside Blanket is the all-important and ever-essential, light and fluffy blanket for keeping warm and toastie.

YARN

| Size | 89 x 100cm |
| | 35 x 39¼in |

Rowan Kid Classic
| A Pink (819) | 7 x 50g |
| B Red (847) | 4 x 50g |

NEEDLES

1 pair of 5mm (US 8) needles.

TENSION

17 sts and 28 rows = 10cm (4in) square measured over pattern stitch using 5mm (US 8) needles.

BLANKET SQUARES

Using 5mm (US 8) needles and yarn A, cast on 21 sts.
Work in patt as follows:
Rows 1 and 2 Using yarn A, *K3, P3, rep from * to last 3 sts, K3.
Rows 3 and 4 Using yarn B, *K3, P3, rep from * to last 3 sts, K3.
Rows 5 to 32 As rows 1 to 4, 7 times.
Rows 33 and 34 As rows 1 and 2.
Cast off.
Work 62 more squares in same way.
Mark RS of each square so that front and back of blanket will be consistent.

MAKING UP

Press all pieces very lightly on WS using a warm iron over a damp cloth.
Arrange squares in an alternating sequence 7 squares wide by 9 squares long, ensuring that the RS are together (see pages 108 and 109). Backstitch all seams.

BORDER

Using 5mm (US 8) needles and yarn A, cast on 5 sts and work as follows:
Row 1 K to end.
Row 2 K2, yon, K3.
Row 3 K4, yon, K2.
Row 4 K3, yon, K4.
Row 5 K5, yon, K3.
Row 6 Cast off 4 sts, K to end.
Rep rows 1 to 6 until border fits neatly around edge of blanket, easing around corners.
Cast off.

FINISHING

Pin border to blanket and backstitch it into place.
Press all seams very lightly on WS with using a warm iron over a damp cloth.

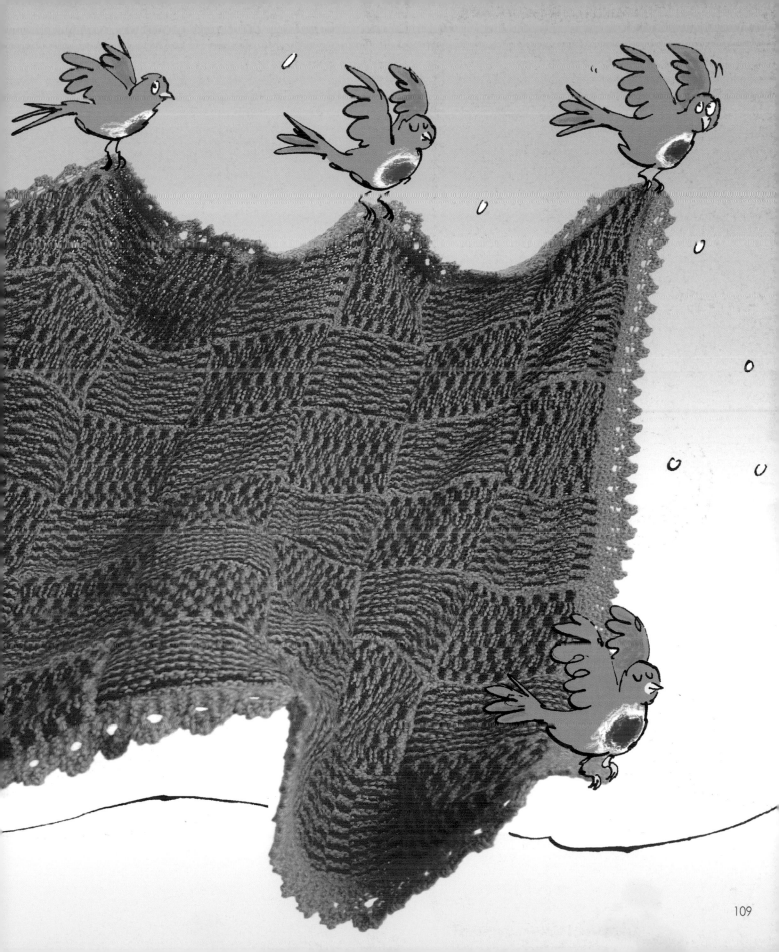

KNITTING TECHNIQUES

ABBREVIATIONS

The following are the standard abbreviations used in the knitting patterns in this book. Any special abbreviations used in a pattern are given with the pattern.

alt	alternate
beg	begin (ning)
cm	centimetre (s)
cont	continu (e) (ing)
dc	double crochet (US single crochet)
dec	decreas (e) (ing)
foll	follow (s) (ing)
g st	garter stitch (K every row)
in	inch (es)
inc	increas (e) (ing) ; in row instructions work into front and back of stitch
K	knit
m	metre (s)
meas	measure (s)
mm	millimetre (s)
oz	ounce (s)
P	purl
patt	pattern
psso	pass slipped st over
rem	remain (s) (ing)
rep	repeat (ing)
rev st st	reverse stocking stitch (purl RS rows, knit WS rows)
RS	right side (s)
sl1	slip one stitch onto right-hand needle
st(s)	stitch (es)
st st	stocking stitch (knit RS rows, purl WS rows)
tbl	through back of loop
tog	together
WS	wrong side (s)
yd	yard (s)
yon	yarn over needle
0 (zero)	no stitches, times or rows for that size

GARMENT SIZES

When working a particular size of a garment, note that the first figure given is for the smallest size; the figures for the larger sizes appear in parentheses. Where there is only one figure it applies to all sizes. Be sure to follow the figures for your chosen size throughout.

COLOURWORK KNITTING

There are two main methods of working with more than one colour in a piece of knitting — the intarsia and Fair Isle techniques. Intarsia produces a single thickness of fabric and is usually used where a colour is only required in a particular area of a row and is not used across the whole row, as with the Fair Isle technique.

Intarsia

The easiest way to work the intarsia technique is to cut short lengths of yarn for each motif or area of colour. When changing colours in the row, link one colour to the next by twisting the yarns around each other on the wrong side to avoid gaps in the knitting. All loose ends can either be darned in later, or can be woven into the back during the knitting process. Weaving-in the ends while knitting is done in the same way as weaving-in yarns when working Fair Isle style knitting, and saves time darning-in ends later.

Fair Isle type knitting

When two colours are worked repeatedly across a row, strand the yarn not in use loosely across the wrong side of the knitting. If you are working with more than two colours, strand the floating yarns as if they were one yarn. Spread the stitches to their correct width to keep them elastic. For the best results, do not to carry the floating yarns over more than three stitches at a time, but weave them under and over the colour you are working, catching them in on the wrong side of the work.

YARN INFORMATION

The following list covers all of the Rowan yarns used in this book. All the information was correct at the time of publication, but yarn companies change their products frequently and we cannot absolutely guarantee that the shades or yarn types used will be available when you come to use these patterns.

   The yarn descriptions here will help you find a substitute if necessary. If substituting yarn, always remember to calculate the yarn amount needed by metrage/yardage rather than by ball weight.

Note Although care instructions for yarns are given here, always refer to the yarn label to confirm care recommendations, in case they have changed since the publication of this book.

ROWAN COTTON GLACE

Yarn type A medium-weight cotton yarn.
Fibre content 100 per cent cotton.
Ball size 50g/1¾oz; approximately 115m (126yd) per ball.
Recommended tension 23 sts and 32 rows to 10cm (4in) measured over st st using 3.25–3.75mm (US sizes 3–5) needles.
Care Machine washable on wool cycle in up to 40°C (104°F) water; do not bleach; dry flat, out of direct heat and sunlight (do not put in dryer); press with a warm iron only; dry-cleanable in certain solvents.

ROWAN 4PLY SOFT

Yarn type A lightweight wool yarn.
Fibre content 100 per cent merino wool.
Ball size 50g/1¾oz; approximately 175m (191yd) per ball.
Recommended tension 28 sts and 36 rows to 10cm (4in) measured over st st using 3.25mm (US size 3) needles.
Care Machine washable on wool cycle in up to 40°C (104°F) water; do not bleach; dry flat, out of direct heat and sunlight (do not put in dryer); press with a warm iron only; dry-cleanable in certain solvents.

ROWAN KID CLASSIC

Yarn type A medium-weight mohair-mix yarn.
Fibre content 70 per cent lambswool; 26 per cent kid mohair; 4 per cent nylon.
Ball size 50g/1¾oz; approximately 140m (153yd) per ball.
Recommended tension 18–19 sts and 23–25 rows to 10cm (4in) measured over st st using 5–5.5mm (US sizes 8–9) needles.
Care Hand wash only; do not bleach; dry flat, out of direct heat and sunlight (do not put in dryer); press with a cool iron only; dry-cleanable in certain solvents.

ROWAN WOOL COTTON

Yarn type A medium-weight wool/cotton blend yarn.
Fibre content 50 per cent merino wool; 50 per cent cotton.
Ball size 50g/1¾oz; approximately 113m (123yd) per ball.
Recommended tension 22–24 sts and 30–32 rows to 10cm (4in) measured over st st using 3.75–4mm (US sizes 5–6) needles.
Care Machine washable on wool cycle in up to 40°C (104°F) water; do not bleach; dry flat, out of direct heat and sunlight (do not put in dryer); press with a cool iron only; dry-cleanable in certain solvents.

BUYING YARN

For the best results, always use the yarn specified in you knitting pattern. Below is the list of overseas distributors for Rowan and Jaeger handknitting yarns. For countries not listed, contact the main office in the U.K. or the Rowan website (www.knitrowan.com).

AUSTRALIA
AUSTRALIAN COUNTRY SPINNERS, 314 Albert Street, Brunswick, Victoria 3056.
Tel: (03) 9380 3888.

BELGIUM
PAVAN, Meerlaanstraat 73, B9860 Balegem (Oosterzele).
Tel: (32) 9 221 8594.
E-mail: pavan@pandora.be

CANADA
DIAMOND YARN, 9697 St Laurent, Montreal, Quebec, H3L 2N1. Tel: (514) 388 6188.

DIAMOND YARN (TORONTO), 155 Martin Ross, Unit 3, Toronto, Ontario M3J 2L9.
Tel: (416) 736 6111.
E-mail: diamond@diamondyarn.com
www.diamondyarns.com

DENMARK
DESIGNVAERKSTEDET, Boulevarden 9, Aalborg 9000. Tel: (45) 9812 0713.
Fax: (45) 9813 0213.

INGERÍS, Volden 19, Aarhus 8000.
Tel: (45) 8619 4044.

SOMMERFUGLEN, Vandkunsten 3, Kobenhavn K 1467. Tel: (45) 3332 8290.
E-mail: mail@sommerfuglen.dk
www.sommerfuglen.dk

ULDSTEDET, Fiolstraede 13, Kobenhavn K 1171.
Tel/Fax: (45) 3391 1771.

ULDSTEDET, G1, Jernbanevej 7, Lyngby 2800.
Tel/Fax: (45) 4588 1088.

GARNHOEKEREN, Karen Olsdatterstraede 9, Roskilde 4000. Tel/Fax: (45) 4637 2063.

FRANCE
ELLE TRICOT, 8 Rue du Coq, 67000 Strasbourg.
Tel: (33) 3 88 23 03 13. www.elletricote.com
E-mail: elletricot@agat.net

GERMANY
WOLLE & DESIGN, Wolfshovener Strasse 76, 52428 Julich-Stetternich. Tel: (49) 2461 54735.
E-mail: Info@wolleunddesign.de
www.wolleunddesign.de

HOLLAND
DE AFSTAP, Oude Leliestraat 12, 1015 AW Amsterdam. Tel: (31) 20 6231445.

HONG KONG
EAST UNITY CO LTD, Unit B2,
7/F Block B, Kailey Industrial Centre,
12 Fung Yip Street, Chai Wan.
Tel: (852) 2869 7110. Fax (852) 2537 6952.
E-mail: eastuni@netvigator.com

ICELAND
STORKURINN, Laugavegi 59, 101 Reykjavik.
Tel: (354) 551 8258. Fax: (354) 562 8252.
E-mail: malin@mmedia.is

JAPAN
PUPPY CO LTD, T151-0051, 3-16-5 Sendagaya, Shibuyaku, Tokyo. Tel: (81) 3 3490 2827.
E-mail: info@rowan-jaeger.com

KOREA
DE WIN CO LTD, Chongam Bldg, 101, 34-7 Samsung-dong, Seoul. Tel: (82) 2 511 1087.
E-mail: knittking@yahoo.co.kr
www.dewin.co.kr

MY KNIT STUDIO, (3F) 121 Kwan Hoon Dong, Chongro-ku, Seoul. Tel: (82) 2 722 0006.
E-mail: myknit@myknit.com

NEW ZEALAND
ALTERKNITIVES, PO Box 47961, Ponsonby, Auckland. Tel: (64) 9 376 0337.
E-mail: knitit@ihug.co.nz

KNIT WORLD, PO Box 30 645, Lower Hutt.
Tel: (64) 4 586 4530. E-mail: knitting@xtra.co.nz

THE STITCHERY, Shop 8, Suncourt Shopping Centre, 1111 Taupo. Tel: (64) 7 378 9195.

NORWAY
PAA PINNE, Tennisvn 3D, 0777 Oslo.
Tel: (47) 909 62 818.
E-mail: design@paapinne.no
www.paapinne.no

SPAIN
OYAMBRE, Pau Claris 145, 80009 Barcelona.
Tel: (34) 670 011957.
E-mail: comercial@oyambreonline.com

SWEDEN
WINCENT, Norrtullsgatan 65, 113 45 Stockholm. Tel: (46) 8 33 70 60.
E-mail: wincent@chello.se
www.wincent.nu

U.K.
ROWAN YARNS, Green Lane Mill, Holmfirth, West Yorkshire HD9 2DX, England.
Tel: +44 (0)1484 681881.
Fax: +44 (0)1484 687920.
E-mail: vintagestyle@knitrowan.com
www.knitrowan.com

U.S.A.
ROWAN USA, c/o Westminster Fibers Inc, 4 Townsend West, Suite 8, Nashua, NH 03063.
Tel: +1 (603) 886 5041/5043.
E-mail: rowan@westminsterfibers.com

ACKNOWLEDGEMENTS

Many thanks to all at Rowan who made this book possible. Eva for her marvellous knitting and pattern writing, Stella for her pattern checking, Sally for her editing and to Susan for all her help and guidance!
Huge thanks to François for his fantastic illustrations and for making the book look gorgeous.